THE TAO
OF SYMBOLS

James N. Powell

THE TAO
OF SYMBOLS

QUILL

New York 1982

For Dave, Joy, and C.

Library of Congress Cataloging in Publication Data

Powell, James Newton.
  The Tao of Symbols.

  Includes bibliographical references and index.
    1. Signs and symbols.   2. Languages—Philosophy.   I. Title.
P99.P64   1982b   001.51   82-5383
ISBN 0-688-01351-1   AACR2
ISBN 0-688-01354-6 (pbk.)

Printed in the United States of America

5   6   7   8   9   10

BOOK DESIGN BY SALLIE BALDWIN

5

Preface

I have no particular ax to grind in the pages that follow other than the notion that the tree I would fell is the very wood of the ax handle in my hands. I have therefore elected to settle in this fast-rooted and dancing tree rather than chop it down, and have no grand theory to defend or solution to offer—only a few chirps of melody and a flock of unlikely juxtapositions (variations?) by poets as laconic as stars. Wherever possible, technical terms have been avoided. More technical treatments of some of these topics can be found in Jan Gonda's *Vedic Literature*, Raimundo Panik-kar's *Mantramañjari: The Vedic Experience*, and Harold Coward's *Bhartṛhari*.

I would like to thank Lisa Ulrich for her frog-lore, Lora Ricca for her assistance in research, Betty Jason for her many valuable contributions, and Ellen Goolsby for her attentive care in the preparation of the manuscript. Also, I would like to thank David Hanks and Merv Lane for their shamanizing, Ann Marie Spargur

7

for her freethinking, Barry Osborne for his kindness, John Powell for his concrete advice, and Jonathan Shear for his helpful suggestion for organizing this material. I would like to thank especially my editors for their careful attention to the full scope of this project.

—JAMES N. POWELL
Santa Barbara, California
May 1, 1982

Contents

Introduction 13
Prelude: Teaching a Stone to Talk
  by Annie Dillard 19
The Labyrinth 29
DA: The Cow Becomes Lightning,
  Frogs, and Flutes 47
Druids 65
Kên: Keeping Still, Mountain 101
Yak 113
Mu 127
Tyger 155
Kiva 179
Cante Hondo 207
The Stone, the Star, and the Oak 231

9

Notes   241
List of Illustrations   247
Index   251

With hands covering his ears, he steals the bell.

—Zen saying

Behold, a sacred voice is calling you; All over the sky a sacred voice is calling.

—Black Elk Speaks

Life's nonsense pierces us with strange relation.

—Wallace Stevens

Ill. 1

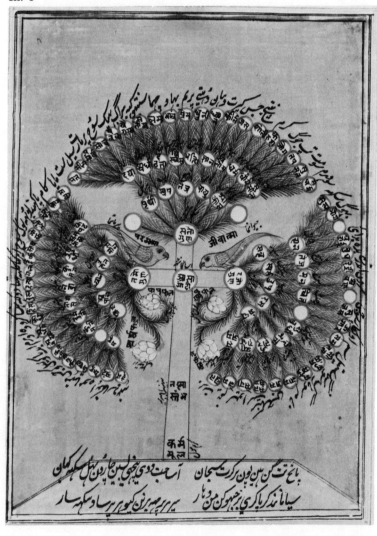

Introduction

God is the Light of the heavens and the earth;
the likeness of His Light is as a niche
wherein is a lamp
(the lamp in a glass,
the glass as it were a glittering star)
kindled from a Blessed Tree,
an olive that is neither of the East nor of the West
whose oil wellnigh would shine, even if no fire touched it;
Light upon Light.[1]

Jutting up abruptly from the desolate Saudi Arabian desert, just beyond the holy city of Mecca, there towers an enormous, barren rock riddled with clefts and caves. It is known as Mount Hira. Just before the sixth century of our era, a young man of twenty-five years often stole away from the city in the dark Arabian night to fast and meditate in a cave on the mountain. One night it seemed as if a joyful peace filled the whole desert, and as the young man lay on the floor of the cave in deepest contemplation the Angel Gabriel appeared before him in a vision of celestial light, commanding, "Cry out!"

"What shall I cry out?" asked the terror-stricken young man trembling. And the answer resounded:

Cry out—in the name of the Lord!
Who created man from clots of blood.
Cry out! For the Lord is most kind,
Who hath by the pen taught humanity
Things it knew not.[2]

The young man continued to visit the cave, and the divine words continued to resound, branding themselves on his soul. He went into the city, cried out the words, and soon gained a following. His disciples recorded these revelations, destined to be heard around the world. For the man's name was Muhammad, the words revealed to him have come to be known as the Koran, and the mountain on which he heard them is today sacred to the millions of followers of the Islamic faith.

Another rock in the holy city of Mecca, the sacred Black Stone, is believed to have been sent down from Heaven by God in ancient times. It is housed within a mountainous stone building known as the Kaaba. The Black Stone is the very hub of the Islamic world, and five times each day, wherever on the globe they may be, devout Muslims face toward this stone, bow down, and intone the name of God, Allah.

Late in 1979, in the enclosure surrounding the Black Stone, a strange event took place. The Iranian revolution had stirred up a number of Islamic groups. One of these was a band of urban guerrillas that, with a storm of machine-gun fire, took over the Most Sacred Mosque containing the Black Stone. Some of the leaders of Saudi Arabia immediately jumped to the conclusion that the Iranians were responsible. Hearing of this, Iran's Ayatollah Khomeini shifted the blame to the Americans and Israelis, who he felt were plotting to turn Muslims against each other. Catching word of this rumored plot, Muslims in Pakistan, Libya, and other countries stormed the American embassies and other institutions within their own borders. The Americans quickly countered that the alleged plot was only a rumor spread by Soviet agents in the Islamic world in order to arouse anti-American sentiment.

With the aid of the French, the Saudis eventually captured the intruders. The guerrillas belonged to an Islamic cult whose motivations apparently had nothing to do with international politics. Yet, when all was said and done, the affair had unintentionally succeeded in inflaming violent sentiments among some dozen nations. All this, ironically, was made possible by a quiet young man and his visions of God's holy Word. And so it is that visions, and the eternal beings to whom they are dedicated, have a strange power over us. They are, in the words of Robinson Jeffers,

> the phantom rulers of humanity
> That without being are yet more real than what they are born of, and
>   without shape, shape that which makes them:
> The nerves and the flesh go by shadowlike, the limbs and the lives
>   shadowlike, these shadows remain, these shadows
> To whom temples, to whom churches, to whom labors and wars, visions
>   and dreams are dedicate.[3]

Symbols—visions, dreams, myths, languages, philosophies, theories—are they content to remain mere phantoms, or do they become as tangible as human flesh? And do not minds, bodies, and weapons then become their very nerves, flesh, and limbs? When armies clash, it is not tank against tank, bomb against bomb, and man against man, but flag against flag, God against God, and symbol against symbol. Thus our relationship to symbols, and the many perspectives to which they give rise, can no longer be viewed as mere child's play or even as intellectual indulgence, but must be appreciated as serious, necessary, and even urgent study.

Yet when we begin to inquire into that relationship, we immediately find ourselves held captive, for it is *with* symbols themselves that we must conduct our inquiry. Thus we are forced to wonder what sort of knowledge symbols are capable of yielding about themselves. Are we eternally confined to the futile activity of thinking about thoughts, verbalizing about words, and theorizing about theories? Or is there in the very *nature,* or what we might call the Tao, of symbols a vision so immediate, so intimate, and so bright that we are blind to it—a vision in which the clamor of conflicting theories, thoughts, and words yields to the deep harmony and silence of the Word?

To be human is to be in dialogue; and while it is comfortable for us to think and converse in our native tongue, to share belief in a theory, or to worship in our hearts a common divinity, such dialogue holds us captive, bewitching us like a jealous God. And all too often, our God is the Demon of our equally bewitched neighbor. One of the great problems of our time, then, is that often our dialogue, and thus our humanity, breaks down due to the seeming mutual exclusivity of these frameworks of thought, these phantoms compelling us to imagine, think, speak, and behave in certain ways. This work speaks of the bewitchment of our dialogue, the bewitchment of our language, and thus the bewitchment of the human mind, which finds its dwelling within language.

Yet in poetry, prayer, and meditation we find language opening to new realms, raising our dialogue from the level of mere communication of often conflicting data to the harmony of deep communion—to genuine giving and receiving. It is in these domains that we find ourselves in touch with something that challenges and transcends all frameworks and thus revitalizes and softens all dialogue.

This work, then, speaks also of the emancipation of our dialogue, our language, and our minds—of how, louder than the firing of machine guns and the accusations of nations, the silence of the central stone, the point around which all these events turn, resounds.

Ill. 2

Prelude:
Teaching
a Stone to Talk

by Annie Dillard

The island where I live is peopled with cranks like myself. In a cedar-shake shack on a cliff is a man in his thirties who lives alone with a stone he is trying to teach to talk.

Wisecracks on this topic abound, as you might expect, but they are made, as it were, perfunctorily, and mostly by the young. For in fact, almost everyone here respects what Larry is doing, as do I, which is why I am protecting his (or her) privacy, and confusing for you the details. It could be, for instance, a pinch of sand he is teaching to talk, or a prolonged northerly, or any one of a number of waves. But it is, I assure you, a stone. It is—for I have seen it—a palm-sized, oval beach cobble whose dark gray is cut by a band of white which runs around and, presumably, through it; such stones we call "wishing stones," for reasons obscure but not, I think, unimaginable.

He keeps it on a shelf. Usually the stone lies protected by a square of untanned leather, like a canary asleep under its cloth.

Larry removes the cover for the stone's lessons, or, more accurately, I should say for the ritual or rituals they perform together several times a day.

No one knows what goes on at these sessions, least of all myself, for I know Larry but slightly, and that owing only to a mix-up in our mail. I assume that, like any other meaningful effort, the ritual involves sacrifice, the suppression of self-consciousness, and a certain precise tilt of the will, so that the will becomes transparent and hollow, a channel for the work. I wish him well. It is a noble work, and beats, from any angle, selling shoes.

Reports differ on precisely what he expects or wants the stone to say. I do not think he expects the stone to speak as we do, and describe for us its long life and many, or few, sensations. I think instead that he is trying to teach it to say a single word, such as "cup," or "uncle." For this purpose he has not, as some have seriously suggested, carved the stone a little mouth, or furnished it in any way with a pocket of air which it might then expel. Rather—and I think he is wise in this—he plans to initiate his son, who is now an infant living with Larry's estranged wife, into the work, so that it may continue and bear fruit after his death.

Nature's silence is its one remark, and every flake of world is a chip off that old mute and immutable block. The Chinese say that we live in the world of the ten thousand things. Each of the ten thousand cries out to us precisely nothing.

God used to rage at the Israelites for frequenting sacred groves. I wish I could find one. Martin Buber says, "The crisis of all primitive mankind comes with the discovery of that which is fundamentally not-holy, the a-sacramental, which withstands the methods, and which has no 'hour,' a province which steadily enlarges itself." Now we are no longer primitive; now the whole world seems not-holy. We have drained the light from the boughs in the sacred grove and snuffed it in the high places and along the banks of sacred streams. We as a people have moved from pantheism to panatheism. Silence is not our heritage but our destiny; we live where we want to live.

The soul may ask God for anything, and never fail. You may ask God for his presence, or for wisdom, and receive each at his hands. Or you may ask God, in the words of the shopkeeper's little gag sign, that he not go away mad, but just go away. Once, in Israel, an extended family of nomads did that. They heard God's speech and found it too loud. The wilderness generation was at Sinai; it witnessed there the thick darkness where God was: "And all the people saw the thunderings, and the lightnings, and the noise of the trumpet, and the mountain smoking." It scared them witless. Then they asked Moses to beg God, please, never to speak to them directly again. "Let not God speak with us, lest we die." Moses took the message. And God, pitying their fear, agreed. And he added to Moses, "Go say to them, *Get into your tents again.*"

It is difficult to undo our own damage, and to recall to our presence that which we have asked to leave. It is hard to desecrate a grove and change your mind. The very holy mountains are keeping mum. We doused the burning bush and cannot rekindle it; we are lighting matches in vain under every green tree. Did the wind once cry, and the hills shout forth praise? Now speech has perished from among the lifeless things of earth, and living things say very little to very few. Birds may crank out sweet gibberish and monkeys howl; horses neigh and pigs say, as you recall, oink oink. But so do cobbles rumble when a wave recedes, and thunders break the air in lightning storms. I call these noises silence. It could be that wherever there is motion there is noise, as when a whale breaches and smacks the water—and wherever there is stillness there is the still small voice, God's speaking from the whirlwind, nature's old song and dance, the show we drove from town. At any rate, now it is all we can do, and among our best efforts, to try to teach a given human language, English, to chimpanzees.

In the forties an American psychologist and his wife tried to teach a chimp actually to speak. At the end of three years the creature could pronounce, in a hoarse whisper, the words "mama," "papa," and "cup." After another three years of training she could whisper, with difficulty, still only "mama," "papa," and "cup." The more recent successes at teaching chimpanzees American Sign Language are well known. Just the other day a chimp told us, if we can believe that we truly share a vocabulary, that she had been sad in the morning. I'm sorry we asked.

What have we been doing all these centuries but trying to call God back to the mountain, or, failing that, raise a peep out of anything that isn't us? What is the difference between a cathedral and a physics lab? Are they not both saying Hello? We spy on whales and on interstellar radio objects; we starve ourselves and pray till we're blue.

I have been reading comparative cosmology. At this time most cosmologists favor the picture of the evolving universe described by Lemaître and Gamow. But I prefer a suggestion made years ago by Paul Valéry. He set forth the notion that the universe might be "head-shaped." To what is the head listening, what does it see, of what does it think? Or is the universe and all it contains a snippet of mind?

The mountains are great stone bells; they clang together like nuns. Who shushed the stars? A thousand million galaxies are easily seen in the Palomar reflector; collisions between and among them do, of course, occur. But these collisions are very long and silent slides. Billions of stars sift among each other untouched, too distant even to be moved, heedless as always, hushed. The sea pronounces something, over and over, in a hoarse whisper; I can't quite make it out. But God knows I've tried.

At a certain point you say to the woods, to the sea, to the mountains, the world, Now I am ready. Now I will stop and be wholly attentive. You empty yourself and wait, listening. After a time you hear it: there is nothing there. There is nothing but those things only, those created objects, discrete, growing or holding, or swaying, being rained on or raining, held, flooding or ebbing, standing, or spread. You feel the world's word as a tension, a hum, a single chorused note everywhere the same. This is it: this hum is the silence. Nature does utter a peep—just this one. The birds and insects, the meadows and swamps and rivers and stones and mountains and clouds: they all do it; they all don't do it. There is a vibrancy to the silence, a suppression, as if someone were gagging the world. But you wait, you give your life's length to listening, and nothing happens. The ice rolls up, the ice rolls back, and still that single note obtains. The tension, or lack of it, is intolerable. The silence is not actually suppression; instead, it is all there is.

We are here to witness. There is nothing else to do with those mute materials we do not need. Until Larry teaches his stone to talk, until God changes his mind, or until the pagan gods slip back to their hilltop groves, all we can do with the whole inhuman array is watch it. We can stage our own act on the planet —build our cities on its plains, dam its rivers, plant its topsoils— but our meaningful activity scarcely covers the terrain. We don't use songbirds, for instance. We don't eat many of them; we can't befriend them; we can't persuade them to eat more mosquitoes or plant fewer weed seeds. We can only witness them—whoever they are. If we weren't here, they would be songbirds falling in the forest. If we weren't here, material events such as the passage of seasons would lack even the meager meanings we are able to muster for them. The show would play to an empty house, as do all those stars that fall in the daytime. That is why I take walks; to keep an eye on things. And that is why I went to the Galapagos Islands.

All of this becomes especially clear on the Galapagos Islands. The Galapagos Islands blew up out of the ocean, some plants blew in on them, some animals drifted aboard and evolved weird forms —and there they all are. The Galapagos are a kind of metaphysics laboratory, almost wholly uncluttered by human culture or history. Whatever happens on those bare volcanic rocks happens in full view, whether anyone is watching or not.

What happens there is this, and precious little it is: clouds come and go as well as the round of similar seasons; a pig eats a tortoise or doesn't eat a tortoise; Pacific waves fall up and slide back; a lichen expands; night follows day; an albatross dies and dries on a cliff; a cool current upwells from the ocean floor; fishes multiply, flies swarm, stars rise and fall, and diving birds dive. The news, in other words, breaks on the beaches. And taking it all in are the trees. The palo santo trees crowd the hillsides like any outdoor audience; they face the lagoons, the lava lowlands, and the shores.

I have some experience of these palo santo trees. They interest me as emblems of the muteness of the human stance in relation to all that is not human. I see us all as palo santo trees, holy sticks, together watching everything that we watch, and growing in silence.

In the Galapagos, I didn't notice the palo santo trees for a long time. Like everyone else, I specialized in sea lions. My shipmates and I liked the sea lions, and envied their lives. Their joy seemed conscious. They were engaged in full-time play. They were all either fat or dead. By day they played in the shallows, alone or together, greeting each other and us with great noises of joy, or they took a turn offshore and body-surfed in the breakers, exultant. By night on the sand they lay in each other's flippers and slept. My shipmates joked, often, that when they "came back," they would just as soon do it all over again as sea lions. I concurred. The sea lion game looked unbeatable.

But, a year and a half later, I returned to those unpeopled islands. In the interval my attachment to them had shifted, and my memories of them had altered, the way memories do, like part-colored pebbles rolled back and forth over a grating, so that after a time those hard bright ones, the ones you thought you would never lose, have vanished, passed through the grating, and only a few big, unexpected ones remain, no longer unnoticed but now selected out for some meaning, large and unknown.

Such were the palo santo trees. Before, I had never given them a thought. They were just miles of half-dead trees on the red lava sea cliffs of some deserted islands. They were only a name in a notebook: "Palo santo—those strange white trees." Look at the sea lions! Look at the flightless cormorants, the penguins, the iguanas, the sunset! But after eighteen months the wonderful cormorants, penguins, iguanas, sunsets, and even the sea lions had dropped from my holey heart. I returned to the Galapagos to see the palo santo trees.

They are thin, pale, wispy trees. You walk among them on the lowland deserts, where they grow beside the prickly pear. You see them from the water on the steeps that face the sea, hundreds together small and thin and spread, and so much more pale than their red soils that any black-and-white print of them looks like a negative. Their stands look like blasted orchards. At every season they all seem newly dead, pale and bare as birches drowned in a beaver pond—for at every season they look leafless, paralyzed, and mute. But, in fact, you can see during the rainy months a few meager deciduous leaves here and there on their brittle twigs. And hundreds of lichens always grow on their bark in overlapping explosions which barely enlarge in the course of the decade, lichens pink and orange, lavender, yellow, and green. The palo santo trees bear the lichens effortlessly, unconsciously, the way they bear everything. Their multitudes, transparent as line drawings, crowd the cliffsides like whirling dancers, like empty groves, and look out over cliff-wrecked breakers toward more unpeopled islands, with their freakish lizards and birds, toward the grieving lagoons and the bays where the sea lions wander, and beyond to the clamoring seas.

Now I no longer concurred with my shipmates' joke: I no longer wanted to "come back" as a sea lion. For I thought, and I still think, that if I came back to life in the sunlight where everything changes, I would like to come back as a palo santo tree, one of thousands on a cliffside on those godforsaken islands, where a million events occur among the witless, where a splash of rain may drop on a yellow iguana the size of a dachshund, and ten minutes later the iguana may blink. I would like to come back as a palo santo tree on the weather side of an island, so that I could be, myself, a perfect witness, and look, mute, and wave my arms.

The silence is all there is. It is the alpha and the omega. It is God's brooding over the face of the waters; it is the blended note of the ten thousand things, the whine of wings. You take a step in the right direction to pray to this silence, and even to address the prayer to "World." Distinctions blur. Quit your tents. Pray without ceasing.[4]

Ill. 3

The Labyrinth

The golden Buddhas pay no heed at all
To pigeon droppings in their raftered hall.

—Ho-o[5]

During the closing millennia of the last Ice Age, teeming herds of powerful grazing mammals swarmed in waves across the vast openness of the landscape, individual animals occasionally falling prey to hunting tribes that depended upon them for food, clothing, and tools. This was the era of the Great Hunt, an age before humans learned to till the soil, and when not only their physical needs, but also their myths, art, and sacred chants centered on the activities of the herds.

Some ten thousand years later, on July 20, 1914, Count Henri Bégouën and his three sons were walking across his property at Montesquier-Avantes, Ariège, France, in the Pyrenees Mountains. It was a hot day, and seeking a cool spot to rest on their outing, they were directed by a local peasant to the *trou souffleur,* an opening in the earth from which a cool breeze wells up. Having found the spot, they became curious as to its depth, and one of the brothers descended into the hole with the aid of a rope. Some sixty feet below the surface the cave led off in a horizontal direction. Leaving behind a trail by unwinding a ball of twine, he crawled along the passageway and made a remarkable discovery. He found a subterranean shrine unseen for some ten thousand years. The walls were alive with magnificent forms— bison, mammoth, rhinoceros, wild horse, reindeer, bear, musk-ox— and towering over all, some fifteen feet above the floor of the cave, in a dancing pose, with an antlered head, the alert, erect ears of a stag, the flowing tail of a horse, and yet the beard and general bearing of a man, there peered down the mysterious Sorcerer of Les Trois Frères. Here reigned a figure half-beast and half-man— one of the most entrancing symbols of paleolithic culture—a silent, eloquent expression of man's oneness with his fellow creatures.

Ill. 4

Yet this is a fleeting oneness; the very images of the Sorcerer and the beasts, in the same sacred act of uniting the human and the animal domains, irrevocably separate them. For no animal laboriously lowers itself sixty feet into a cavern, crawls along awkwardly on its belly through a narrow passage leading to a subterranean chamber, and there worships magnificent images that it has reverently painted on a wall. In the very act of symbolically uniting himself with the animal world, the artist transcends and displays dominion over it.

We humans, it seems, are fond of comparing our intelligence with that of the other members of the animal kingdom. We gossip, go to church or to the moon, hit our fingers with hammers, spend money, and have wars—all of which help lend us that special dignity that divides us from the mere beast. We remind ourselves of this superiority by calling ourselves social animals; cultural animals; animals that speak; religious, economic, tool-making, and technological animals. We want to remain apart from the beasts.

On the other hand, if an ape picks up a rock and uses it in a toollike fashion, we feel a sudden affinity; and each year we expend countless sums trying, as Annie Dillard put it, "to raise a peep out of anything that isn't us." We wish to be distinct from, but also to be one with, the other animals—to live and speak with them. In earlier eras we danced about with horns attached to our hats, and etched drawings of bison on the walls of caves. For unlike our modern Western way of emphasizing the physical and material realm, archaic humanity was ultimately concerned with the spiritual dimension. To enter into this realm was to step *into*, rather than out of, reality. And often it was the vision of an animal that guided an individual into this realm. When hunting was a holy activity, a spiritual understanding and union between hunter and hunted was believed to take place before the actual slaying. In the same way an observant man might court a woman, the hunter knew through certain divinations and clues that the creature had surrendered in spirit. Through the power of rituals—songs, dreams, and cave paintings—the hunter knew he had secured permission to take the animal's flesh as a gift. In such paintings, in which no bison would recognize an image of itself, we betray our uniqueness; it is here we find a clue to that activity which separates us from the beasts—the activity of symbolizing. The human animal is, if nothing else, the symbolizing animal, and it is the act of symbolizing that is not only most characteristic but also most fundamental to human intelligence.

Our display of symbolization is almost limitless. We use sounds to communicate, and call this our language. We use mathematical symbols to solve complex problems involving relations between things. We listen to music, enter sacred buildings, and bow before images. If a bird appears to bow before a statue of the Buddha, it is only bending to peck away a few grains of sacrificial rice, which have been offered there by members of the symbol-using set. If the Buddha does not bow back to the bird, there are no hurt feelings. The bird is almost equally unaware of the statue as anything special. If we use symbols, we are also used by them, as when we march blindly to our destruction in the footsteps of a flag bearer. And we are also capable of totally transcending symbols (or of seeing to their essence), capable of the jeweled quiescence of the Buddha.

We may be tempted to object at this point that animals do respond to symbols. And it is true that, to a degree, they seem to. The human distinction of being the symbol-user is merely a matter of degree. Some researchers believe whales and dolphins have the ability to communicate—to a degree. Moreover, we have taught chimpanzees and gorillas to use sign language and other modes of communication, but again it is a matter of degree. After all, the most eloquent primate does not begin to approach the fluency of a normal child, and we would have a hard time finding a gorilla that would go to church or shell out cash to go to a movie, to buy a Picasso, or to buy a book. We would have a difficult time finding a tiger that would starve itself to death rather than eat a cow, which it deemed especially holy. Human beings eat bananas, but we don't style ourselves the banana-eating animal. Gorillas, on the other hand, spend entire days consuming whole banana trees, one after another, from the leaves and fruit on down to the roots. It is a matter of degree, and they might well earn the title.

Therefore, if we exclude nonhuman primates and other mammals from the designation of symbol-users, it is only because they do not appear to be as involved with symbols as humans. They use symbols to a degree but, like their fellow members of the animal kingdom, spend a great deal of time responding to *signs* rather than *symbols*. For instance, a dog may hear verbal signals, such as a call for feeding. But it is clear that the animal hears in such utterances only *immediately* pragmatic and directive meanings. The dog directs its senses and actions to something *immediately present* in the environment. An utterance is a mere *signal,* like a green traffic light, signifying something to be done or noticed instantly, a stimulus for action rather than a medium for reflection and mental exploration.

Animals possess only a crude sort of code book, a small vocabulary of signals designed to elicit a stereotyped response. The territorial cry of a bird is taken by other birds as a direct, immediate, emotionally charged warning. Their response to it is immediate and rigidly fixed in their genetic makeup. Humans, on the other hand, are capable of creating an infinite number of sentences from a much larger vocabulary. I say, "Koala bears have a difficult time digesting caviar and oysters," and anyone who knows English knows what the sentence means, though it may never before have appeared in the entire history of the universe. Moreover, each spoken sentence may elicit a totally unpredictable, nonstereotyped response: you ask a Zen master the meaning of Zen, and he hits you with a stick. Nor is human language necessarily emotionally charged. We are quite capable of thinking of the meaning of a sentence apart from its emotional content, and so we can write volumes of scientific prose. Most animals seem unable to distinguish between the message and the emotion. When a dog barks it is angry. A human, however, may speak pleasingly even when angry, or may program computers with emotionally dead information.

Another unique aspect of human language is its capacity to allow us to roam far away in spirit—to wander into the past, the future, the realm of the galaxies or that of the atoms. We can imagine, remember, think, meditate, and have an awareness of time. Dogs and rats, on the other hand, can remember a signal only for a brief instant. It goes in one ear and out the other.

As humans, then, we possess two languages—an external, social one, like the fixed signals of animals, and an inner one. Thus while some animals are certainly capable of a crude form of dialogue, most are quite incapable of soliloquy, contemplation, and all the other activities of the inner language, at least to the degree that we indulge in these.

It is within this interior language that we break away from the fixed outer language. The reason that philosophies, poetic styles, and theories remain in vogue only briefly is that we are capable of going within ourselves and seeing there novel ways of rearranging the way in which words link up with things. In this way, poetic eras begin in revolution, become accepted as convention, and finally deaden into cliché and boredom, only to be replaced by a new poetic vision. And it is in this way that suddenly Albert Einstein was able to join together two things in the physical universe—matter and energy—in an entirely novel manner, with an equal sign. $E = mc^2$. Matter *is* energy. And our universe has not been quite the same since.

Thus while humans may respond to signs in the same manner as animals, our relationship to signs is not limited to an automatic, genetically fixed response. We see the sky becoming cloudy, hear thunder, and know these to be *signs* of an impending thundershower. We run for shelter. On the other hand, we are capable of talking about thunderstorms even when it is quite sunny.

There are, of course, many kinds of symbols—linguistic, musical, graphic, dream, mathematical, and so forth. In fact, we cannot even engage in what we normally call thought without symbols—for it is not the case that we have a thought and then seek words to express it. Rather, we think only in terms of our language, and our language is composed of symbols. Even when we think in pictures or sounds instead of words, these form a language of their own. And since we constantly think, we really dwell *within language.* Now consider for a moment that though the vocabulary of the average person may be larger, he or she will use from it roughly the same hundred words on an everyday basis. We exist, then, in a cage of some few hundred words, a set of clichés; the limits of what we can say determine the boundaries of what we can think. The typical farm boy in Iowa, for instance, has a very limited way of describing waves in the ocean. A dedicated California surfer, however, lives in a world of water and wind conditions that are either glassy, blown out, choppy, off-shore, onshore, or flat. Where the surfer sees and talks about shore breaks, beach breaks, point breaks, reef breaks, peaks, sections, lefts, rights, lines, sets, tunnels, bowls, tubes, shoulders, lips, backs, troughs, curls, swells, slop, slosh, glass, juice, and so on, the farm boy sees only waves and a beach.

Not only is our day-to-day vocabulary confining, but we are forced to speak it in the unvarying grammar of our language. "The boy sees the tree," we say. Subject, verb, object—and with minor variations and few exceptions we paint with words a certain picture of the world in which we dwell. This is a world painted as if it were composed of objects like apples and tables, qualities like red and green, and actions like walking, sitting, and slurping. This is a world, in other words, of nouns, adjectives, and verbs, with a few minor parts of speech stuck in to glue these basic building blocks together.

Nature is a continuity, which we might represent by a line:

But our language tells us that the world is made up of "things" that we have named. Those aspects of the world that we do not name have little or no existence for us. Our named world, in contrast to the continuity of nature, looks like a broken line:

The lines represent the named "things" and the spaces are those aspects of reality that remain without names, and that do not exist for us. For the farm boy from Iowa, the lines may represent such words as "ocean," "beach," "breaker," or "comber." He simply does not see the fine distinctions that the surfer appreciates. All the terms the surfer uses to describe and move about in his world are, for the farm boy, merely blank spaces, a world that does not exist.

In this way a speaker of Chinese or Swahili paints a totally different picture of the world than a speaker of English. The lines and the spaces fall in different places. The Hopi Indians paint a picture very much like the one painted by the mathematical language of modern physics, a subject we will return to in a later chapter.

We dwell, then, not so much within a physical world made up of atoms as within a picture of that world painted by the units of our language. In fact, it was the Greeks who first gave us our concept of atoms, and when Democritus, a native of Abdera in Thrace, said that matter is made up of atoms, the model he used to demonstrate his point was the way in which sentences are made up of their parts.

The human mind, then, imagines, conceives, muses, meditates, thinks, dreams, and compares in manifold symbolic forms of language. And if this is so, what are the general laws that govern all these activities? Or perhaps there is just one general law, one Tao, that underlies all our symbolizing, being the very *nature* of symbols. In order to reveal the Tao, or nature, of symbols, let us look first to the growth of those mathematically formalized symbolic constructs known as scientific theories.

The development of scientific thought appears to be guided by two tendencies. One of these we may call empirical adequacy. This is the demand that scientific theories link up with and correspond to observable facts. Newton's theory of gravity was, we are told, brought home to him by an observable apple that landed on his equally observable head. The other tendency we may call integrated generality. This prompts scientific language to move toward higher, more general, more abstract, usually mathematically formulated levels of expression. Newton did not just say that an apple landed on his head; he used language that was more general, more abstract, in fact mathematically elegant. He said, $G = k\frac{mm'}{r^2}$, a sentence in the language of science, which is both highly abstract and highly general. It describes not only the falling of an apple through the atmosphere, but also the falling of planets in their orbits about the sun.

These two tendencies act upon each other in such a way that in the evolution of science, theories tend to explain more and more facts, connecting with nature at more and more points, while simultaneously moving toward more abstract, more general expressions. A crude example might be that of an ancient nomadic herdsman who suddenly realizes that two cows and two cows add up to four cows. After some thought, the herdsman may comprehend that, similarly, two pails of milk and two more make four, and so on. The two tendencies dictate that eventually the general and abstract statement $2 + 2 = 4$ will emerge. Compared with the expression "Two cows and two cows is four cows," the statement $2 + 2 = 4$ is both more empirically adequate, linking up with an infinite number of observable facts, and more abstract. It integrates the description of the vast realm of observable facts into one concise mathematical expression. Eventually the statement "The whole is equal to (or more than) the sum of its parts" will emerge—a statement that is both more empirically adequate and more general and abstract than its predecessors, for it speaks of *any* sum.

Scientific theories tell stories about things in the universe. Old scientific theories are not so much replaced as they are taken into the more inclusive language of a more general story about the universe. These stories, like fishing tales, seem to get more and more fantastic with the passing of time. This, then, is the Tao of science. New theories engulf older ones like the increasingly larger members of a biological food chain. And, again like fishing tales, the larger the story, the larger its subject, whether it be a twenty-five-pound trout or a universe of matter that an especially imaginative "fisherman" tells us is made up of nothing but energy.

Einstein's physics didn't replace Newton's physics so much as it gulped it down, digested it, and assimilated it into a larger story.

The language of science tends to enfold in one abstract expression as much reality as possible. As Einstein, speaking of physics, said, "We are seeking for the simplest possible system of thought which will bind together the observed facts."[6] Thus scientific formulations constitute a kind of language that seeks to make nature intelligible—a language that evolves in the direction of concision, an almost aesthetically appreciated elegance. If a straight line is the entire universe and all of its laws, science tends to want to describe this limitless line with a dot. And we find that symbols display this same tendency wherever they are found.

In the same era when James Clerk Maxwell drew together the previously disparate fields of electricity, magnetism, and light into a unified theory of the electromagnetic field; the era when the separate notions of wave and particle in physics were replaced by a single, deeper, unified concept of wave function that applies to both light and matter; and the era when Einstein's special theory of relativity unified the concepts of space and time, matter and energy into the the concise $E = mc^2$, areas other than physics were becoming increasingly unified by appealing to the power of the simplest, most elegant symbolic expressions. In poetry, for instance, attention shifted from the poem as a whole to the line, the individual word, and even the syllable—and in psychology, concise, abstract dream symbols began to yield worlds of meaning.

In poetry the shift of attention was influenced by nineteenth-century linguistics. With the discovery of resemblances among Sanskrit (the ancient language of India), Latin, and Greek, linguists began to realize that all the "daughter" Indo-European languages were actually dialects of an older "mother" tongue called Proto-Indo-European.

The daughter dialects grew mutually unintelligible through a long process of divergent evolution. It seems that several thousand years ago there lived in the area of the Ukraine, in what is now the Soviet Union, a loose confederation of tribes. For some

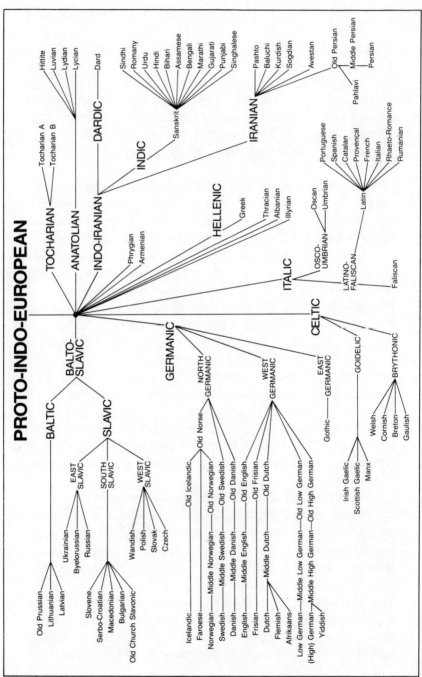

Ill. 5

unknown reason they disbanded and migrated in waves across Europe all the way to Ireland, and south into Iran and India. Today the loose confederation of tribes and the language they spoke are called Proto-Indo-European, and all the daughter tongues that evolved from the latter are called Indo-European languages. These languages have not grown so far apart, however, that there are not considerable resemblances among them. Consider, for example, what a poet might do with the following set of Indo-European words, all grown from the same Proto-Indo-European root:

tantra: Sanskrit for the Indian art of erotic spirituality, a stretching of the senses into the realm of the spirit
tendu: French for the ballet position that is an extension of the thigh and leg
tender: English, of course, for all things gentle, kind, loving, amorous, sympathetic, soft, touching or playful

Words related in such a way are called cognates of one another, for they have a common origin.

Now consider the vast new realms open to the poets who began to benefit from this discovery. Poetry had always been concerned with condensing maximum resonance into minimum space, and now Ezra Pound, T. S. Eliot, and others of their generation began to hear and employ the subtle resonance that each Indo-European word awakens in its cognates. In the previously disparate Indo-European tongues an "echoing intricacy"[7] was suddenly heard. Each language now formed a branch of a newly discovered and enthusiastically explored linguistic tree.

In *The Waste Land,* T. S. Eliot invokes the most ancient literature in an Indo-European tongue by quoting from a venerable old Indian scripture, The Great Forest Teaching (Brihadāranyaka Upanishad). In a passage from this scripture the Lord of All Creatures is instructing all the assembled beings in his creation. His entire instruction consists of a single syllable, DA, which is the sound of thunder. In this one resonant thunderclap is all the wisdom necessary for men and even Gods. For those who do not get the message, however, he gives the following commentary: DA means give *(datta)*, sympathize *(dayadhvam)*, and be self-controlled *(damyata)*. In Sanskrit these three commands each begin with *da*. Thus, for Eliot, speaking to the lost postwar generation, the Word, the voice of God, the thunderclap that contains all the wisdom necessary to correct the spiritual disloca-tion of that generation, is contained in a single syllable, DA. Here we have the integrated generality, the poetic equivalent of Ein-stein's $E = mc^2$, and delivered at the speed of light. In this way the most diminutive elements of the poem gain new possibilities of meaning.

While enchantment with this Indo-European "echoing in-tricacy" was reaching its efflorescence, a visual resonance, via Pound's fascination with Chinese ideograms, began to emerge in his poetry. Thus on the many-branched linguistic tree in full bloom flowered the lotus, and along with it the opportunity to condense into the visually compact Chinese ideogram ever more densely vibrant meaning. In the line

$$日 昇 東$$

"Sun rises (in the) east," we are given a picture of what actually takes place in nature. On the left we find the shining sun, on the right is the sun as seen through the branches of a tree, and in the middle we see the sun just above the horizon. In Chinese script the painting of the world that is given in language becomes clearly graphic as soon as it is written down.

This discovery of the East by Pound and Eliot provided an orientation adopted later, and variously, by such American poets as Charles Olson, Robert Duncan, Gary Snyder, and Allen Gins-berg, who were deeply influenced by Pound's ideogrammatic style and those most minimal of Eastern linguistic forms *mantra, sūtra, haiku,* and *koan*. We will discuss these forms in later chapters. In poetry, as in science, the tendency to illumine as much reality as possible by means of the most elegant, concise expression prevails.

As poetry sometimes reminds us, our symbol-using activities are not limited to the waking state of consciousness, for even while asleep we spontaneously produce symbolic images of the most fantastic variety in the form of dreams. With the pioneering work of Freud and Jung these symbols were seen to possess a logic and meaning, to form a language that, interpreted correctly, opens the way to a therapeutic understanding and resolution of conflicts. Again, in psychology, as in physics and poetry, the tendency of this language to embrace as much reality as possible displays itself. Dream symbols, through a quality that Freud called condensation, are capable of combining in a single image or concise series of images a montage of interlocking patterns of meaning. In this way they attempt to make conscious and resolve what previously remained unconscious.

For Freud these images signified conflicts having the dreamer's personal history, specifically childhood experience, as their origin. Jung, however, postulated deeper dream images that present and unfold an awesomely more vast reality, including not only the personal past of the dreamer but the entire collective consciousness of humanity. In these images, which he called archetypes, appear figures and motifs that are found all over the globe. One archetype is the anima, or female within the male. If the dreamer is a man, he will find that a female figure appears within his dreams. If he is wise enough to heed her, she will act as a guide, just as Beatrice guides Dante or the Lady in the garden guides T. S. Eliot in his poem *Ash Wednesday.*

A striking example is found among the shamans of the Eskimos. These spiritual tricksters, psychopomps, and healers often wear women's garments. In addition, we have the story of a young man who was being initiated by an older shaman. The old man buried the boy in the snow. Shivering with cold, the boy had a vision in which a woman appeared, emitting light. She gave him all the instructions he needed in order to become a great shaman and acted as his guide throughout his life. Jung believed that if a man does not find this inner female guide, he will seek her outside of himself, always looking to be mothered and protected by an outside force, whether this is an actual person, an institution, or a nation. The individual must learn that he possesses all the wisdom of the anima within himself. Only then can he relate to women, and to men, in a genuine manner. And again, we see that in Jung's theory a single, abstract symbol connects with reality in myriad forms. For the anima is really formless, an abstract archetype that can take any female form.

Symbols, then, have become focal. High-energy physics no longer deals with observable things. The behavior of subatomic phenomena can be interpreted only through the symbols of the language of mathematics. In psychology, the unveiling of subconscious material depends also on interpretation of the symbols of dream language. Because of this, Western thinkers have begun to assert that the human being is indeed the symbol-using animal. We have realized that every human activity, every Tao, every path or way—be it the path of physics or prayer, the way of dream analysis, poetry, music, painting, or meditation—is a way of symbols. It is now evident that understanding of the human mind will increasingly rely upon an understanding of the symbols with which it is so indissolubly united, especially linguistic symbols. It is not only the farm boy from Iowa who is linguistically bound to a limited view of the waves; the philosopher is in the same boat. Different philosophical views of the world, we have discovered, may be as dependent upon language as are the varying views of the same ocean by the farm boy and the surfer. As Hugh Kenner aptly observes:

One senses that Hegel was possible only in German, and finds it natural that Locke in a language where *large* and *red* precede *apple* should have arrived at the thing after sorting out its sensory qualities, whereas Descartes in a language where *grosse et rouge* [large and red] follows *pomme* [apple] should have come to the attribute after the distinct idea.[8]

Thus two philosophers, reflecting upon the same apple in differing languages, see different apples in ways determined by the structures of their languages. Such realizations led philosophers in general to become increasingly concerned with language, and

Wittgenstein in particular to proclaim that we are as if held captive by the picture painted by language. He asserted that the true task of philosophy is to free the mind from the bewitchment of language. For whenever we make any statement, we paint a picture of the world, and that picture is linguistically bound. Especially when making the most meaningful of statements, in religion and philosophy, we find ourselves running up against language in every instance.

Symbols, especially linguistic symbols, have become focal. They offer poetic prowess, mathematical abstractness, "echoing intricacy," or the ability to create, make conscious, condense, communicate, and universalize. Yet studies of symbols only emphasize the labyrinthine contours of the human mind, within the chambers of which presides a consciousness that is always, like the man-animal of Les Trois Frères, a hybrid—a man-symbol, a man-language. We are inseparable from, bewitched by, language—and seemingly without any means of overcoming this enchantment.

Ill. 6

DA:
The Cow Becomes
Lightning,
Frogs, and Flutes

Becoming lightning, the cow has thrown back the veil.

—RIGVEDA

Deep silence enjoys an eloquence of its own, and we can say little without diminishing it. In the poetry of Kabir, a fifteenth-century Indian lover of God, this silence seems to sing of itself:

Near your breastbone there is an open flower.
Drink the honey that is all around that flower.
Waves are coming in:
there is so much magnificence near the ocean!
Listen: Sound of big seashells! Sound of bells![9]

Deep within the poet's breast toll sounding shells, sounding bells, sweetness, an inner squall of quiet thunder . . . Silence flowers into sound, audible to the poet listening deeply. In this way the silence that few hear becomes a poem by Kabir, audible to all.

Some thousand years before Kabir penned these lines, the ancient Indian bard who bequeathed to us The Great Forest Teaching heard that same inner thunder. However, rather than describing the experience in terms of the sounds of seashells and bells, he spoke of DA, which sounds like thunder to Indian ears, just as "moo" sounds like a cow to ours. As we have seen, this voice of thunder was the utterance of the Lord of All Creatures, summing up in a single, resounding syllable how the blinding knot of egoity is to be unraveled. All the scriptures and sacred codes of behavior we find in India are only the audible echoes of this silent thunder.

Long before the appearance of India's great scriptures, as the glaciers of the last Ice Age began to retreat, the vast grasslands bordering them shrank in the shadow of waves of forest trees, advancing northward like great armies from their warm areas of refuge to the south. Immense pastures simply disappeared, and the herds of grazing animals began to diminish. These animals, which had previously been followed by hunters, were gradually domesticated, yielding not only meat and leather but also milk. Thus they provided both food and clothing, and in at least one nomadic culture, the cow became the very symbol of perfect giving. This was the Indian branch of the great Indo-European tribes. As these people drifted through the mountain passes into India's Ganges Plain, there emerged a culture in which linguistics, philosophy, poetics, and religion were not yet divided into separate, proudly autonomous fields, each with a name, a department, professors, Xerox machines, and a few students—rather the entire fabric of knowledge was seen to be woven within a single syllable.

At the very heart of this culture lay one of the most fascinating of all literatures, the poems, chants, riddles, and *mantras* of the Vedas.[10] "Veda" means "wisdom" or "knowledge." According to tradition, this wisdom is eternal, sacred, and not of human authorship. The Vedas were handed down with impeccable fidelity not in writing, but by a disciplined chain of oral recitation. The transmission of these sacred words, with exact precision, became a holy duty—for should a syllable or accent be overlooked or misplaced, it could unleash a terrible power. The grammarian Patañjali tells of a demon whose name was Indrashátru, Conqueror of Indra. Now this demon retired from active life and devoted himself to intense meditation. As a result the Creator appeared before him, saying that because of his piety he would be granted a wish. The demon thought for awhile, and then simply asked that Indrashátru should prosper. However, he made one slight mispronunciation. He said "Indrashatru," which without the accent means "Whose Conqueror Is Indra." Thus through his own wish, faulty only in the omission of a single accent, he perished.

The reason for maintaining the fidelity of the Vedas was that although it was believed the Vedas were eternal and had always existed, they were revealed *visually* to seers. The Vedas were thought to be *seen* by sages or poets *(rishis)* whose intuitive, transcendental power of vision was beyond the limitations of time and space, free from error, and thus capable of receiving and transmitting the timeless Vedic wisdom without distortion.

Their visions were sudden, lightninglike flashes of illumination imparting an instantaneous realization of truth. In fact, to be wise in Vedic society was to possess poetic vision, to command a power of *seeing* truths hidden beyond the empty meanderings of the external eye.

The verses of the Vedas seen by these sage-poets describe the process of seeing. More than that, they were thought capable of revealing the luminous domain from which they issued. Vedic poetics was an exact science performed by a community of sacrosanct master poets concerned with the expression of deep intuitive truths in precise poetic statements—so precise, in fact, that they give rise to an invariable experience. This four-thousand-year-old art-science contains a knowledge of profound linguistic subtleties that will contribute enormously to the current Western concern with language as the key to understanding the symbol-using animal.

If we merely understand the Vedas in terms of the prejudices inherent in our own concept of language, we may succeed in fitting these ancient revelations into a comfortable framework; but if we do so, the subtlety and beauty of these utterances will escape us. We must be willing to enlarge our concept of language far beyond our present experience. For our ordinary notion of the inner dimension of language includes only the realm of thought, reflection, and other forms of mentation—but in India the understanding of inner language is much more profound. For the seer, language is divine, the Goddess embracing the entire universe.

According to Vedic tradition, the human mind is something like a field containing seeds that, given the right conditions, are eager to sprout. These innate seeds are of two kinds—those that cause ignorance, unhappiness, and suffering and those that lead to enlightenment. The sounds and images of the Vedas awaken those seeds which lead to happiness, direct perception of reality, and enlightenment—giving rise to specific inner experiences and increasingly enlightened mental states along the way. The art-science of Vedic poetics blooms deep within one's own consciousness. The knowledge of the Vedas is not *really* knowledge until it becomes one's own knowledge—lived rather than understood intellectually. Interpretations of and commentaries on the Vedas are useful, then, only insofar as they describe the enlightening nature of Vedic language and the conditions under which it reveals its own meaning.

It is natural for Vedic passages to appear quite opaque to the intellect, for the level of meaning they awaken far transcends the ordinary boundaries of our minds.

Words, like tools, have different purposes, and Vedic utterances are *mantras,* literally "mind-tools," instruments for probing the most subtle strata of consciousness, for locating the visionary furnace in which all words are forged. They are not, then, bearers of information. As Wittgenstein said of poetry in general, "Do not forget that a poem, even though it is composed in the language of information, is not used in the language-game of giving information."[11] We must, therefore, look to the *use* of these utterances, these mind-tools, rather than to their intellectual import. Their meaning and verification are not in what they *describe,* but in the depth of consciousness they expose. And *mantras* have been used for centuries in India to probe deeply into consciousness. They appear to be sheer nonsense; yet when used therapeutically, as instruments to awaken innate, enlightening images and states, they reveal their own meaning. If we treat them as statements, as what philosophers call propositions, we are doomed to miss the point. After all, how does one analyze a line of Vedic verse that is pure sound, with as little intellectual import in Sanskrit as in English:

Hābu hābu hābu hā ū hā ū hā ū.

Or what is the intellect to do with the following passage: "Becoming lightning, the cow has thrown back the veil."

Vedic utterances, then, are objects not of intellection but of meditation, and provide a means of discovering hidden depths of reality. These riddles and instruments do not present us with information and ideas, but with images and sounds that embody deep intuitions. They are verbal icons, maps that delicately zero in on visionary domains, with the fleet precision of a hawk and the illuminative power of a nuclear warhead. When the physicist J. Robert Oppenheimer witnessed the blinding radiance of the first atomic blast, he thought of a vision of the Lord found in an ancient Indian scripture:

If the light of a thousand suns
Should suddenly burst forth in the sky
The radiance would be like
The light of the Exalted One.

Meditation on Vedic verses becomes a kind of game language plays with itself in order to release its own inner energies—a riddling that answers itself striking from abysmal depths—as when you are walking quietly on a mountain path and suddenly a snake jellies beneath your bare foot. All of a sudden there is no path, and no mountain. There is only the void, and you spring into it with the leaping, uninvented intelligence of a frog jumping into a pond, or a cow becoming lightning.

The Vedic tribes were agricultural and seminomadic, and cattle breeding was a central part of their lives. Early each morning the herds were driven from their stalls to pastures where they roamed freely and grazed. One of the most common scenes in Vedic life must have been that of mother cows mooing to their calves and nursing them. This picture of maternal affection is, in fact, one of the focal images of the Vedas. Through this image the seers suggest their experience of language. For them, the riddle or *mantra* is a cow.[12] When in meditation the riddle cracks, the flash of poetic vision that floods the mind is a cow flowing with a thousand streams of luminous milk. Thus everything that happens to cows in the Vedas is an algebraic symbol of what happens to language.

The moment of poetic vision and the instant of creation of the entire universe are one and the same; the world leaps forth with the Word. The seers sing of this creation:

In the beginning, before creation, all the elements are present. The cows, the Sun, the waters, and the light of the dawn are all there, but in a concealed, veiled state. There is no orderly *flow* to the universe. Everything is held back by Vritra, the Covering. Vritra is the veil or obstruction that holds back the perfect flow of creation. Indra, the Bright One, is a liberator. He appears to fight with Vritra, who conceals the waters, the cows, the dawn, and the Sun within a mountainous Stone in his belly. Indra heats himself for battle, drinks three vats of sweet Soma, and with his thunderous lightningbolt kills Vritra, bursting the demon's belly and the Stone, and thus releasing, like milk from a huge udder, the lowing cows, the sonorous rivers, the light of the dawn, and the Sun. He props apart Heaven and Earth, and the *flow* of creation is released.

This entire tale describes, in veiled imagery, the process of Vedic visionary poetics, especially the four levels of language that the seers called the Word. Just as in The Great Forest Teaching the entire precept on overcoming egoity is implanted in a single seed syllable, DA, the total wisdom concerning the four levels of language is in the Sanskrit root *kshar*—"to flow." From *kshar* comes the word *a-kshara*, which means "nonflowing," "immutable," "eternal." *Akshara* is the innermost core of language and of the universe.

THE LANGUAGE OF ETERNITY (AKSHARA)

The Vedic seers speak of a plenum of inner silence, so full that within its quietness it contains everything—all sounds and forms. All aspects of language, and thus all the elements of creation, are somehow enfolded within this stillness—though in a pristine aphony prior to form, which has yet to unfold and sonorously flow into pure configuration.

In the tale of Indra and Vritra the elements of language and creation, curled within the Nonflowing, are called the cows, the waters, the dawn, and the Sun. They are trapped within the mountainous Stone in Vritra's bowels, and getting them to burst radiantly forth is something like getting this Stone to talk. Vritra, the Veil or Covering, must somehow be removed. The state of the Word here is like a mother cow whose udder is swollen to the bursting point with the bright milk of poetic vision, and the entire universe is about to flood forth.

The knowledge of the Vedas is neither the words we read in books, nor the thoughts of them we have in our minds. It is this inmost, tumescent stillness, this swollen silence. It is not even knowledge, but pure knowingness, crystalline consciousness intimately in touch with itself. Here there is no object of knowledge or perception, no thought—simply boundless, blissful awareness, innocently in awe of its own boundlessness. It is still yet moving, silence swimming within silence.

Somehow this pure, curled aphonia begins to unfurl, opening like the cupped, luminous membranes of a shell to radiant configurations that are the inner foundations of language and of the universe. The flower within the breast blooms, tolling with the sound of bells, the deep resonance of the sea, and, we might say, the sound of a cow becoming lightning.

THE LANGUAGE OF THE SOUND-LIGHT CONTINUUM (KSHĪRA)

"Becoming lightning, the cow has thrown back the veil." It is only at a distance that we see lightning and then, in direct proportion to that distance, hear thunder. If we, like the cow or some wizard, could actually *become lightning*, we would know that between our luminosity and our sonority there is no distance. The two are one for us and only two for someone at a distance.

Since there is no distance between language and human consciousness, since our awareness is so intimately infused with language that the two cannot be distinguished, we can, like the cow, become transformed into lightning-thunder. For the cow in the Vedic verse above is language, and lightning is the level of language that we will call the flash of poetic vision, the language of the sound-light continuum.

When language is in its purest, inmost state—what we have called the Nonflowing, the language of eternity—our awareness is also eternal. When this silent level of speech explodes into vision it is as if we become lightning.

Lightning is the perfect image to use as a verbal icon of this interior state; it echoes the burst of luminous sonority, the bright bellowing cow, of poetic vision. This cow, in the very act of becoming lightning, has unveiled the deep brilliance of the Word. For this reason the seer of The Great Forest Teaching simply used DA, the sound of thunder, to represent the voice of the Father of All Creatures striking down the knot of egoity. This inner sounding, though silent, is, as a more modern seer expresses it, "the primal sound which, sounded at the beginning, resounds in every portion of the Vedas, which are nothing but echoes of this."[13] It is the silent voice of divinity, which must be not only heard but *seen*, the Word within the word, that heartfelt resonance which lends integrity to all action. The instant it is truly heard-seen, the ceaseless self-obsession of the ego is calmed.

Besides using the images of bellowing cows and rolling thunder, the Vedas symbolize this inner sound by speaking of sonorous rivers, roaring fires, howling winds, croaking frogs, and resonant musical instruments. In meditation these images move toward that immovable, mooing silence as surely as seashells echo the thundering waves.

The poets of later eras in India compared the inner thunder

to the ocean, waterfalls, or swarms of love-mad bees. Or the inner domain of language is Lord Krishna's flute, echoing throughout his boyhood home. This music enchanted the milkmaids in the region, causing them to abandon their chores, children, and even husbands to flee to the forest and dance to the music. All of creation becomes blissful upon hearing the melodiousness of the flute. Clouds hover like huge cows, shedding sweet drops of moisture. Rivers flow past more slowly that they might hear the sound, and lotuses blossom wantonly on their sensuous stems, intoxicated with the tunes. Even the Gods become senseless, contemplating in their hearts the divine melodies. In paintings Lord Krishna is often depicted playing his flute to an admiring herd of cows. And that interior flute was heard by at least one admiring poet. Kabir sings:

At last the notes of his flute come in,
and I cannot stop from dancing around on the floor. . . .

The blossoms open, even though it is not May,
and the bee knows of it already.

The air over the ocean is troubled,
there is a flash, heavy seas rise in my chest.

Rain pours down outside;
and inside I long for the Guest.

Something inside me has reached to the place
where the world is breathing.

The flags we cannot see are flying there.
Kabir says: My desire-body is dying, and it lives![14]

Another of Kabir's poems that expresses luminosity in sound is this next song:

The flute of interior time is played whether we
hear it or not,
What we mean by "love" is its sound coming in.
When love hits the farthest edge of excess, it reaches a wisdom.

And the fragrance of that knowledge!
It penetrates our thick bodies,
it goes through walls—
Its network of notes has a structure as if a million suns were arranged
  inside.
This tune has truth in it.
Where else have you heard a sound like this?[15]

In its most elegant, condensed form, the sum total of Indian wisdom is found not in riddles of thunder or cows, or in the poems of Kabir, but in a single resonant syllable such as the mind-tool *(mantra)* Om. Om is the entire universe, proclaims an ancient Indian scripture; and it is also Vedic poetics in its most concise, elegant form. If it seems like nonsense, we must remember that $E = mc^2$ seemed like nonsense before it was put to use.

Like lightning, when the still, silent Word thunders, it is simultaneously luminous. Light and sound flow forth in bright concert. The Vedic poets were called seers precisely because the Word, when experienced on very refined levels, is luminous. As the cow becomes lightning, luminous, silently thunderous rivers of sweet poetic vision flood into the being of the seer. These are rivers of the milk of the cow of language. This is why we have used the word *kshīra,* or "milk," to describe this state. Whereas *akshara* is the nonflowing milk of the Word, *kshīra* is a word that also comes from the root *kshar* and means a *flowing* of milk.

In the tale of Indra and Vritra, the lightningbolt Indra hurls at Vritra *is* the luminous flash of poetic vision, the cow becoming lightning that rends the Stone. Instantly the bright milky rivers, the mooing cows, and the light stream into the vision of the seer. Vritra and the Stone are language concealed. Indra is language revealing language. And the rivers, the light, and the cows are language revealed.

The world unfolds in concert with the Word. This truth is recognized not only in India, but also among the Maori of New Zealand. There the Supreme Being is called Io. Before creation, say the Maori, there was an immense darkness. As Io said:

Let there be light above
Let there be light below
A dominion of light
A bright light[16]

the light appeared. The Maori know that these were the very words, because they were luminously impressed upon the minds of the ancient poets who transmitted them down through the ages. They call these words

The ancient and original sayings
The ancient and original words.
The ancient and original cosmological wisdom
Which caused growth from the void,
The limitless space-filling void,
As witness the tidal-waters,
The evolved heaven,
The birth-given evolved earth.[17]

And these very words, the same incantations that Io used to create light and the world from the void, are used even today to enlighten the mind and inspire the hearts of those who compose songs. New words and new worlds are revealed by the original words.

With the Vedic seers it was much the same. The seer Long Darkness has left us with these lines:

The Cow (the Word) mooed, and the floods came.
Having become one-footed, then two-footed,
Then four-footed, eight-footed and nine-,
She sits in the highest heaven, having a thousand syllables.

From her (the Word) flow the oceans of heaven,
From her the four directions,
From her flows the *akshara*, the nonflowing,
And on this *akshara* the whole universe abides.[18]

The cow, the Word, mooed. The Sanskrit word for "moo" is *mā*—which also means "to measure" or "to build." When the cow moos, when luminous rivers of thunderous language flow, time and space as well as light and sound come into being. It would be more accurate to say that time-space-light-sound comes into being, for they all arrive at once, intermingled. In this embryonic stage of inner language, words as we know them have not yet emerged. A continuum of light-sound reverberates and vibrates with divisions that, though inherent, are not yet articulate, just as the limbs and organs of a human embryo are indistinct. All the syllables and meters of the sacred *mantras,* all the hooves of the cow are pulsing. A thousand nascent syllables, all language is humming, shining, yoked to eternity. The ocean of speech is undivided, bursting to emerge as syllables as surely as the sweetness gathered by bees from an ocean of flowers is placed in multichambered combs. The Word has not yet become words; and only the most abstract impulses of the world, the four directions of space and the metrical divisions of time, are beginning to emerge. Sounds and images are here so intimate with eternity, the Nonflowing, that time-space-sound-light bathes in the infinite as one enormous being.

The Language of Thought (Kshīra)

Kshīra, besides meaning "milk," can also mean "curds"— the curdled milk that can be divided into little bricks of cheese. Like milk, the language of the sound-light continuum is lively with all the nascent divisions of thought. The Word descends from its incandescent throne, arriving in the mind as separate thoughts that are as divisible as cheese. We notice that thoughts pour into our minds ceaselessly from somewhere. We seem, in fact, to be somehow in a mental cage. We think endlessly, never seeing the infinite Word before it arrives in our minds as finite units of language. The task of the Vedic mind-tools is to enlarge our experience of inner language by overthrowing the dominance of thoughts.

THE LANGUAGE OF SYLLABLES (AKSHARA)

Silence, as we have said, contains an eloquence of its own. The silent Word spontaneously finds expression in words; it finds form in poetic verse—in syllables that are uttered in time and that fill up space on a page. *Akshara*, besides meaning "nonflowing," also means "syllable." In one word, then, we can locate the entire spectrum of language, from nonflowing, eternal silence to sounding syllables. Nonflowing silence contains within itself all of language, all syllables. And each syllable contains eternal silence. For the seer who is ever immersed in silence, even while speaking, syllables never cease being silence, and silence is ever full with syllables of inspired speech. The great lovers of God, though they say the experience is inexpressible in words, are some of the world's best poets.

Since each syllable of the Vedas contains this silence, each word contains the Word. Each syllable contains all the Vedas and the sum total of knowledge to be found in all the thousands of syllables that make up the Vedas. Similarly, each image, when it is meditated on, contains all the other images and syllables of the Vedas. As a Vedic scripture teaches:

Speech is the essence of the human mind;
The Rigveda is the essence of speech;
The Samaveda is the essence of the Rigveda;
The single syllable Om is the essence of the Samaveda.[19]

A single syllable contains the entire Vedic revelation. All the *mantras*, odes, riddles, and hymns of praise, and all the divinities to whom they are sung, are enfolded within the most diminutive splinter of speech.

Verse 39 in hymn 164 of the first cycle of the Rigveda tells us that all the divinities dwell within the *akshara*. This can, of course, be interpreted in two ways. All the divinities dwell within silence, abide in the eternal; or they all dwell within a single syllable.

Despite our minds, intellects, powers of reasoning, and intelligence, we remain riddles to ourselves, bound within the laby-

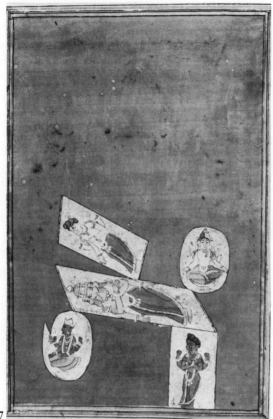

Ill. 7

rinth of language. We cannot step back from language, or leap or fly over it. For it is our own minds, bound in language, that would leap, and the the very sky into which we would escape is but another creation of our thought. Thus we measure out our lives syllable by syllable. We can never really have a knowledge *of* language, but only *in* language. To penetrate *in* language to the center is to find the core of our own being and of the universe. Each syllable measuring out the dimensions of our world is, in essence, measureless—infinite, eternal. In exploring the depth of language we find that the universe is a spoken reality, that the Word speaks through us and through all things.

Our dwelling is within this Word, and the dimensions of that dwelling are precisely equal to the depth of our awareness of that Word. Poetry is a measuring, a fathoming of the vastness of that dwelling. In the highest realm of speech, the dwelling is without limit. This is the summit of the poetic.

When the poetic riddle cracks, revealing its meaning—when the cow moos, becoming lightning—this *mooing* (from the root *mā*) is also a *measuring* (also from the root *mā*), a sounding of the unfathomable.

Language not only reveals but also conceals itself. It weaves illusions that artfully bewitch us. In fact, the seers saw the entire creation as nothing but the mirage-making power of the Word. They had a name for this spell casting—they called it *māyā*, another derivative of the root *mā*.

The nonflowing eternity of the Word is measureless. When it begins to flow, when it moos, a measuring occurs and the beginning of an illusion emerges. The spell of *māyā*, the illusion of measurement, is cast as directions, time, space, and words; and worlds arise from their silent source.

The seers, besides thinking of the Word as a cow, also thought of her as a beautiful woman whose unadorned radiance is revealed only to her lovers. Each syllable of the Vedas, each movement of this Goddess, conceals silence. Yet each syllable is capable of revealing inmost beauty, as a radiant woman sheds her garments. The verses of the Vedas, the sounds and images, like the clothing of a woman, suggest an underlying beauty. The seers warn us, however, that this mistress cannot be forced. She alone reveals herself to those who love her. She is her own authority, requiring no commentary to reveal her greatest mystery. Embracing and transcending Heaven and Earth, she moves in concert with and upholds all the luminous divinities. She grants visions, illumining herself, making her lovers powerful and wise seers. She is at once the diversity of names and forms, and the unity of formless, poetic intuition. She is both communication and communion. She is concealed in the heart and revealed through love and worship.

Among those who love her there is true friendship. Only among those who do not know her fully does she cause struggle and even death. To those who know her intimately, Heaven and Earth are abundant, for she is the essence of the human heart and of the entire creation. Simply by attending to language wisely the entire mystery of creation opens, harmony spreads among the worlds, and each individual finds fulfillment.

Each syllable of the Goddess blooms from inmost silence. Each flowering, each unfolding, is also an enfolding, an embrace. Each blossom enfolds silence, creating a particular sound and form. Each word and object in creation is thus an embrace of the Goddess, opening to eternity. When the indusium of words is lifted, an inward penetration and flowering reveals the most intimate life of the Goddess, the Word.

Ill. 8

Ill. 9

Druids

Innate Ideas. are in Every Man Born with him.

Whatever can be Created can be Annihilated: Forms cannot:
The Oak is cut down by the Ax, the Lamb falls by the Knife,
But their Forms Eternal Exist For-ever. Amen. Hallelujah!

—WILLIAM BLAKE

Not that I want to be a god or a hero.
Just to change into a tree, grow for ages, not hurt anyone.

—CZESLAW MILOSZ[20]

I see us all as palo santo trees, holy sticks, together watching
everything that we watch, and growing in silence.

—ANNIE DILLARD

Which is the tree, which is the forest, from which they have
fashioned Heaven and Earth, stationary, undecaying, and giving
protection to the deities?

—Rigveda

Outside my open window dwells an oak. I seldom really see it; I'm too busy. Yet sometimes, as unexpectedly as a sudden breeze billowing the curtains, it gathers my attention, filling me with its dark presence. It must have spoken to someone else, too, for whoever built this quiet little cottage left a notch in the eaves of the roof, allowing a gray branch to gnarl its way skyward unobstructed. Evidently the architect miscalculated, and the carpenter simply compensated in favor of the oak, disfiguring the roofline rather than the integrity of the living form.

Just down the hill stands another oak, agonized, twisted, yet flourishing. It is framed by a vast window, inside of which hangs a man, carved from oak. He dangles limply from a cross, his back to the window and the great tree. People come to this little stone chapel to dance and sing, to sit quietly, and to pray—sometimes,

I think, more to the tree than to the oaken figure that seems to merge with it.

Oaks abide. And abiding they are revered, for they reveal that which abides within us. What frequenter of oak groves at dusk has not felt the abysmal power of their stillness and borne it secretly away into the night? Oaks abide, and oaks are prayers— their dark hearts leafing outward into the light as surely as human hearts flower inward, following the grain of an even fuller illumination.

Like oaks, words that embody the abiding endure through vast reaches of space and time. In fact, our words "truth," "trust," and "tree" can all be traced back four thousand years to an ancient Proto-Indo-European word for the tree that to them was the Truth. That tree was the oak. They called the oak *dorw, which also meant "firm," "strong," "enduring." The oak is, after all, a stout tree, as anyone who has cut through oakwood can testify.

The word "Druid" is also in the *dorw family. The Druids were a priestly class of bardic seers endowed with visionary powers. The name itself means "seer of oaks," and one wonders what they saw that would give them such a title, for a seer is one who perceives forms not available to the perception of the common eye.

One thing is certain. The oak had a special meaning not only for the Druids, but for the Indo-Europeans as a whole. During the warm period around 2000 B.C., before the dispersal of the Proto-Indo-European tribes, grand oaken forests covered most of Europe, extending hundreds of miles north of their present thermally mandated boundary. Giant oaks, much larger than any present-day specimens, were sources of food (in the form of acorns) and religious inspiration. These trees so impressed the Proto-Indo-European consciousness that the oak became established as the focal religious symbol of that era. Because it revealed the abiding, it was a symbol of great durability and power. In fact, if one traces the descendants of the Proto-Indo-European oak word in the various Indo-European languages, from Ireland to India one finds they are represented prominently in religious usage. This tree was, as we have noted, the Truth.

All the Indo-European High Gods were bearers of the thunderbolt, and were called Thunderers. It is natural that the oak was sacred to each of them, because it is struck by lightning more often than any other tree. It channels the power of the Thunderer to Earth.

Thus the Balts burned fires in sacred oak groves to their God of Thunder. The Teutons ignited holy oakwood fires in honor of Donares eih, their Thunder God. The Greeks felt that sounds coming from the oak were oracular, the voice of Zeus, the Thunder Bearer. The tribes of ancient Italy maintained perpetual oakwood fires, watched over by vestal virgins, and Jupiter was worshiped in the form of an oak. The Celtic Druids ate acorns, worshiped in sacred oak groves, lighted oakwood fires, and praised the Celtic High God in the form of the oak. What was it, we ask again, that these *seers* of oaks saw?

Turning now to India, the Sanskrit relatives of the ancient Proto-Indo-European term for oak *(*dorw)* provide the answer. The most obvious relative is *dāru,* "tree." In ancient cultures trees had not yet come to be valued as board feet of lumber. The tree represented the immeasurable Truth, the Cosmic Pillar, the Axis of the World, extending into Heaven. Around it the entire universe was thought to revolve, just as the constellations circle Polaris, the North or Pole Star. In fact, like the star-crowned Christmas tree, the Cosmic Tree is often depicted in ancient myths and art as crowned with the Pole Star.

When the Aryan tribes spilled over the mountain passes of the Hindu Kush into the fertile river valleys of northern India, they entered an alien climate, leaving behind the great oaken forests of their homeland, far to the north. But they carried with them their language, and with it another relative of **dorw* that retained in its sound and meaning something of the forgotten sacred oaks of their ancestry. The Sanskrit word is *dhruva,* and it means "the abiding, the firm, or fixed one." It is also the name of the star that abides like the oak, the Pole Star, Polaris. And it was *dhruva,* the Pole Star, that became a subject for Patañjali, one of India's greatest seers and teachers. He lived around 500 B.C. and left us a sort of lab manual, the Yoga Sūtras, a work of concise and precise formulas (sūtras) for the systematic unfolding of consciousness (yoga).

The third chapter of this treatise is concerned with subtle, supernatural powers (siddhis). Formula 28 of this chapter states that "by performing samyama on the Pole Star (dhruva), one gains knowledge of the motion of the stars."

Now this seems obvious enough. After all, shepherds, sailors, astronomers, and lovers—in fact, anyone having normal vision and residing in the Northern Hemisphere—has the ability to observe the nocturnal heavens rotating around the North Star. The only perplexity is that Patañjali, a writer of great precision and economy of expression, should list this as a subtle, supernatural power. Perhaps this meditation on the abiding star has something to do with why the Druids were called seers of the abiding tree.

The key to this riddle is the word samyama, which has no equivalent in English. According to Patañjali, however, the term designates a technique of meditation in which three qualities of consciousness merge. These three qualities are (1) the abiding, (2) the flowing, and (3) the uniting.

1. The abiding is fixity or duration of attention on an object. This does not simply mean staring, for even if we stare fixedly at something we experience delicate lapses of attention. This abiding quality is involved in every act of attention, but it seems that objects like stones, the Pole Star, and oaks—or even the ideas of them—are naturally unmoving and have the ability to draw us into the depths of the abiding. In fact, the Sanskrit term for this abiding quality of consciousness is another word derived from the ancient Proto-Indo-European oak word *dorw. The Sanskrit term is dhāranā. As Martin Heidegger said: "To think truly is to confine oneself to a single thought which one day stands still like a star in the world's sky." This standing still of thought is dhāranā.

2. Attention cannot be forcefully fixed upon an object for any great duration. The mind spontaneously flows from one act

of attention to the next. However, if the mind is quiet, peaceful, and thus spontaneously concentrated, it can flow uninterruptedly toward any object. It flows abidingly. Flowing and nonflowing coexist. The Sanskrit term for this flowing quality is *dhyāna,* and it, too, is involved in every act of attention.

3. Finally, when the attention flows so strongly and fixedly toward an object that it abides totally in the object and merges with it, a state of identity or unity with the object is experienced. This is called *samādhi.* In the purest form of *samādhi,* awareness has no object of attention. Consciousness is simply absorbed within its own unbounded, blissful nature. In this state of peace, should the attention be directed toward any object, it would flow toward it and remain fixed in it without effort. This unifying aspect of consciousness is also present, to some extent, in every act of attention.

Saṃyama, again, is the meditation in which these three qualities of abiding, flowing, and uniting merge in a powerful act of attention. They merge to some degree of effectiveness in every act of attention. The goal, then, is not to replace the normal act of thinking with some extraordinary act but, through meditation, to reveal the full intensity and power of which every act of attention is capable at its deepest level. Though Patañjali does not tell us how this technique of *saṃyama* is actually accomplished, something of it can be suggested by a visual analogy.

The starlike diagram on the next page is used in India as an object of meditation. Fixing awareness on it produces a flowing quality. Like an oak, this seemingly static design is capable of revealing profound depths.

Patañjali's formula contains two phrases. There is an instruction: "By performing *saṃyama* on the Pole Star . . ." And there is a predicted result: " . . . one gains knowledge of the motion of the stars." Until recently, we had no way of knowing what Patañjali meant by "knowledge of the motion of the stars." In January of 1981, however, a paper appeared that promises to have far-reaching influence. It presented the results of an experiment performed on the formula in question. The technique of *saṃyama*

Ill. 10

was taught to hundreds of subjects from around the world who were already skilled in meditation. Their experiences were recorded. Dr. Jonathan Shear, who conducted the research, states that taking Patañjali at face value

one would expect to perceive the motion of the stars in the context of the heavens as we are accustomed to perceive and think about them. And in fact such perceptions do represent early phases of the experience produced by the technique in question. But in many cases the experience quickly develops into something quite different. The pole-star is seen at the end of a long, rotating shaft of light. Rays of light come out from the shaft like the ribs of an umbrella. The umbrella-like structure on which the stars are embedded is seen rotating. Along the axis of light are other umbrella-like structures, one nested within the other, each

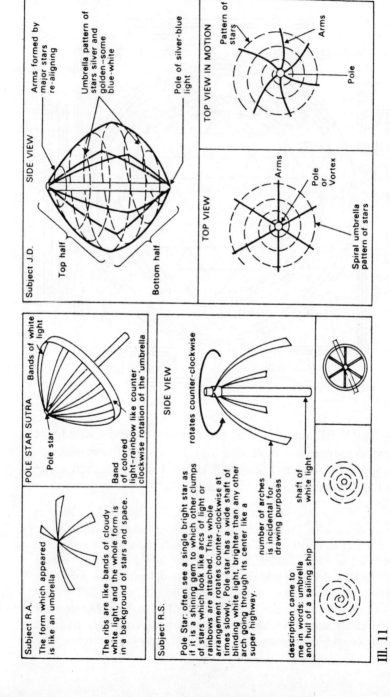

Ill. 11

Examples of Subjects' Sketches of Experiences from the Practice of the "Pole-Star" Sutra of TM-Sidhi Program

Subject R.A.

The form which appeared is like an umbrella.

The ribs are like bands of cloudy white light, and the whole form is in a background of stars and space.

POLE STAR SUTRA   Bands of white light

Pole star

Band of colored light—rainbow like counter clockwise rotation of the 'umbrella

Subject R.S.

Pole Star: often see a single bright star as if it is a shining gem to which other clumps of stars which look like arcs of light or rainbows are attached. This whole arrangement rotates counter-clockwise at times slowly. Pole star has a wide shaft of blinding white light, brighter than any other arch going through its center like a super highway.

number of arches is incidental for drawing purposes

shaft of white light

SIDE VIEW

rotates counter-clockwise

description came to me in words: umbrella and hull of a sailing ship

Subject J.D.

SIDE VIEW

Arms formed by major stars re-aligning

Umbrella pattern of stars silver and golden—some blue-white

Pole of silver-blue light

Top half

Bottom half

TOP VIEW

Arms

Pole or Vortex

Spiral umbrella pattern of stars

TOP VIEW IN MOTION

Pattern of stars

Arms

Pole

rotating at its own rate, each with its own color, and each making a pure, lovely sound. The whole experience is described as quite spectacular, blissful, colorful and melodious.[21]

What is important to note is the precision of Patañjali's expression. The experience described, like the result of any scientific experiment, is repeatable, and is specific to the meditation on the Pole Star formula. Moreover, none of the subjects had any prior knowledge of the structure. They were all taken quite by surprise, for they never imagined that anything of the sort existed until the moment they experienced it. "The experience," says Shear,

is the innocent by-product of the proper practice of the technique. The logical conclusion is that the specific content of the experience represents the mind's own contribution arising in response to the practice of the technique. This is, the technique enlivens specific, non-learned or innate responses, and allows us to experience what can, I think, properly be called an innate archetype or structure of the human mind.[22]

This is an important point, for it demonstrates that no particular result was sought after. The experience was an innocent and spontaneous response of the mind to a given stimulus. Innocence of the mind is of great importance in such inner work, as a Tibetan folktale instructs us. There once lived, the tale begins, a very good and generous man. He was admired and loved by all those who lived in his village. One day a venerable holy man was passing through the village, and the generous man approached saying, "I would like to become enlightened, compassionate and truly wise, for I want to assist all beings to reach enlightenment. Please instruct me."

The holy man instructed the kind man in a certain type of meditation and advised him to go to the mountains and devote himself to it. After some time, he said, if practiced with sincerity, the meditation would lead to enlightenment.

The kind man followed these instructions, retiring to a cave in the mountains. He meditated there for twenty years and absolutely nothing happened. He was not enlightened.

He returned to the village, where the holy man happened to be visiting again. He approached the holy man saying, "For twenty years I have sat on that mountain and meditated in the manner you instructed. Nothing happened. I am not enlightened."

The holy man asked what instructions he had given, and the kind man told him. Upon hearing the kind man's words, the holy man said, "I am very sorry, but what you did was useless. I told you the wrong thing. Now you will never reach enlightenment."

Disheartened, the kind man returned to his cave. He thought that he might as well continue his meditation, since he had been doing it all of these years. There was just one difference, however. He no longer did it for the purpose of reaching enlightenment. He sat to meditate, and enlightenment came immediately. He saw all things clearly and understood that his intense grasping of the concept of enlightenment had prevented him from experiencing it.

Patañjali demonstrates in his *sūtras* the same skill in teaching as the holy man who taught the kind man. Patañjali allows the mind to remain innocent. Shear's research demonstrates the futility of intellectualizing over Indian scriptures or attempting to get at the meaning of a *sūtra* through reasoning and logic. Like the mind-tools *(mantras)*, the formulas *(sūtras)* are instruments for probing consciousness, and their meaning is found in their proper use.

If the experience described by Shear's subjects is innate, inborn—if it is somehow an urgent presence in all human consciousness, bursting to reveal itself—we would expect to find evidence of its eruption in the visions of sensitive souls. We would expect to find it celebrated throughout the world in myth, poetry, and song. And we will see in what follows that this vision is indeed found throughout the world, lending credence to Shear's hypothesis that it is an innate structure of consciousness.

To begin with, ancient Indian collections of legends known as the *Purānas* present descriptions of the universe that correspond to the sketches and accounts provided by Shear's subjects.

The seers of the *Purānas* tell of seven Heavens. They are nested one within the other along a Cosmic Pillar and at the top the Pole Star reigns supreme. In the six lower Heavens, there revolve the Sun, Moon, stars, and planets. These luminaries are bound to Dhruva with fetters made of winds. At the highest point of this celestial structure where the Pole Star resides one finds Dharma, Cosmic Law, all the principles of right action. Now "Dharma" is another relative of the ancient Proto-Indo-European oak word, and a term of prime importance in Indian experience. Dharma is the silent order that upholds all activity in the universe. It regulates the motions of the galaxies and planets, the seasons, and all the activities of nature. It is also the power that upholds all correct behavior in the human sphere and discourages all activity that is wrong. The vision of this structure is of the greatest practical value, for it reveals the still center from which all harmonious action emerges. In India, those saints who are in accord with this silent hub of Dharma are thought to emit a spiritual power that, though unseen, exerts an orderly influence on the environment, freeing it from all kinds of misfortune. Thus the activity of *seeing* this inner axis of the universe was thought to be more important than a million good deeds, for the *seeing* would prevent harmful activities from occurring for miles around. This is why in the East skillful inaction is considered to be a tremendously potent form of action.

Long before the *Purānas* were written down, and long before the time of Patañjali, we find the same vision reported in the Rigveda. We have already quoted Heidegger's statement that "to think truly is to confine oneself to a single thought which one day stands still like a star in the world's sky." The Rigveda provides a similar statement:

On top of the distant sky there stands
The Word, encompassing all.[23]

Dhruva, besides meaning Pole Star, can also signify a cow that stands still while being milked, the Word that stands still in the sky of the mind. The seer Long Darkness tells us of the cow-Word standing at the summit of Heaven flowing with the milk of visionary light. Thus we are presented with an image similar to the one in Patañjali's Pole Star formula, except that in the Highest Heaven we find the Word instead of a star standing still, abiding. When thought abides it can see into the heart of things. The attention of the seer, fixed in the Word abiding in the Highest Heaven, flows with the following vision. He beholds an immense shaft of fire that extends through the entire universe. Along this axle seven celestial wheels revolve, yoked to the pole by spokes. Each wheel makes a separate tone. These seven tones are the songs of seven virgins who dwell in this tree, chanting seven secret words. And at the crown of the structure presides the self-luminous Word. It is said that two birds dwell in the tree. But only one of them is able to ascend to the top and eat the sweet fig there. This symbolism, as we shall see, is found also in archaic Siberian shamanism. When a young shaman is initiated, he or she must ascend a post or tree. To reach the top is to reach the center of the universe and to achieve ecstasy.

According to the seer Long Darkness, language both conceals and reveals this tree. And a more modern poet, Czeslaw Milosz, agrees, commenting that when all is said and done we may muse

> that we lived in a golden fleece,
> In a rainbow net, in a cloud cocoon
> Suspended from the branch of a galactic tree.
> And our net was woven from the stuff of signs,
> Hieroglyphs for the eye and ear, amorous rings.
> A sound reverberated inward, sculpturing our time,
> The flicker, flutter, twitter of our language.[24]

Language is both the net and the rainbow. It is both the cocoon clouding our vision of perfect centeredness and the magical hieroglyphs, amorous rings, and fluttering wings that open and transport us to the still center.

The Axle Tree grew also in ancient Greece, where we find a graphic description by Plato in the myth of Er, which appears near the end of his *Republic.* In this myth Er dies, ascends into

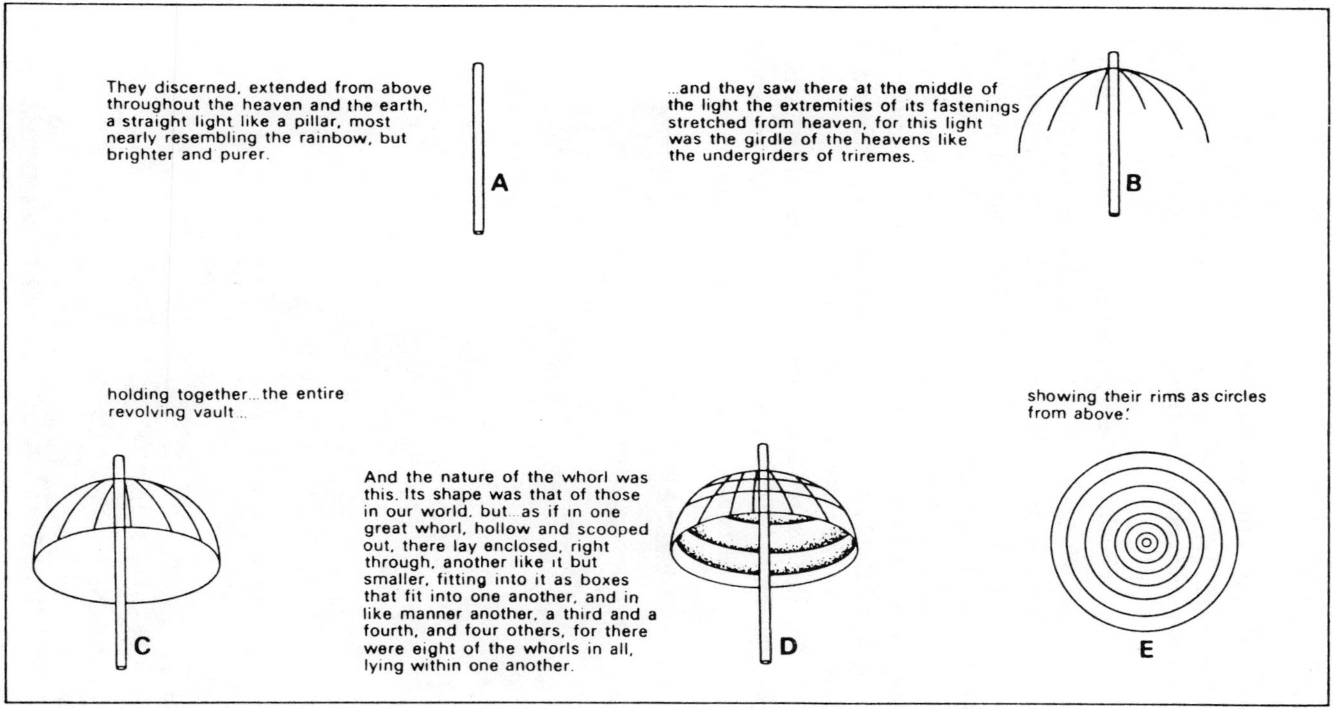

They discerned, extended from above throughout the heaven and the earth, a straight light like a pillar, most nearly resembling the rainbow, but brighter and purer.

A

...and they saw there at the middle of the light the extremities of its fastenings stretched from heaven, for this light was the girdle of the heavens like the undergirders of triremes.

B

holding together...the entire revolving vault...

C

And the nature of the whorl was this. Its shape was that of those in our world, but, as if in one great whorl, hollow and scooped out, there lay enclosed, right through, another like it but smaller, fitting into it as boxes that fit into one another, and in like manner another, a third and a fourth, and four others, for there were eight of the whorls in all, lying within one another.

D

showing their rims as circles from above.

E

Ill. 12

The Structure of the Cosmos Described in The Myth of Er, *Republic*, 616b - e⁴ (with artist's construction from the text).

Heaven, and then returns to his body to tell of his experiences. He speaks of the realm of Ideal Forms, the true and real Forms of which the named objects in the material universe are but pale shadows.

While in the realm of these Forms, Er sees a shaft of light, more luminous than a rainbow, stretching through the universe. At its summit are the fixed stars, and extending from them, the chains of Heaven, luminous belts that hang down attached to large hollow whorls. These fit into one another like bowls. On the upper surface of each circular whorl is a siren hymning a single melodious tone. Shear cites this as evidence that the structure experienced by his subjects is innate, and argues that it is one of the Ideal Forms that Plato described.

Whether the seer resides in India, Greece, or Siberia, when the veil of ignorance lifts, the jeweled tree upon which the whole universe turns appears as a brilliant shaft of light with seven or

Ill. 13

so celestial wheels embracing all the clusters of galaxies. Often it is depicted with one or several birds at its summit representing the ascent of the spirit.

An Australian aborigine would paint an equally recognizable Cosmic Axis, though his pigments and inks might differ. Yet the vision determining the shape of the design would alter as little as the knowledge curled within a seed. As Hugh Kenner, speaking of patterns, observed:

Potent in a rough bluish-brown capsule the size of an acorn lie the forces that know how to shape an Australian Gum Tree and send it rapidly to great heights in a dry climate. In the late 19th century Australia's climate reminded someone of Italy's, and today the gum trees grow here and there by the Mediterranean. A rhymer of climates planted one on a hillside above Rapallo, just where the long steep *salita* down from Sant'Ambrogio turns left for its final descent to the town. Its material, like that of most artifacts, is local: Italian water and Italian air, clasped in a cellulose tension network of which the patterned integrity alone is Australian.[25]

Like local water and local air are the beings of our mythological kingdoms. These heros, unicorns, damsels, dragons, dwarfs, all the luminous pantheons, and Cosmic Trees reign but for an hour. They suffer mutability as surely as Shelley's clouds, "Streaking the darkness radiantly!—yet soon/Night closes round, and they are lost forever." In one mythological instant in one culture it is an oak, in another the Pole Star, or a stone, or a cross, or a statue of the Buddha that becomes the central immovable object of adoration. Although the outer forms may alter, they are contoured by a deep structure, a blueprint for possible universes, which molds thoughts, perceptions, dreams, visions, and actions according to a strictly defined pattern so deeply rooted in awareness that it eludes us. It is as if we hear a splash in a pool but do not see the force that caused it. What we do see is energy spreading away in concentric rings, made visible only by the water. The water through which the energy pushes is different at every instant, yet it must flex in contour to the pulse throbbing through it. Meanwhile, the unseen force abides deep within the myth, poem, dream, or image, an invisible iridescence serenely hidden like a trout waiting deep in the current.

This rainbow tree reveals its iridescence only to the subtle perception of the inner eye, for it is the form of the subtle, divine cosmos from which the material universe and all its forms proceed. It is the inner icon that trees, galaxies, and even the human body are patterned after, so that all these open to the central mystery. Thus the Cosmic Tree painted by our Indian artist bears a striking resemblance to a "tree" called the *sushumṇā*, the Rich in Happiness Tree, which Indian wisdom informs us blossoms within the human body.

Along this tree are located seven vibratory centers called *chakras* or "wheels," just as along the Cosmic Tree there are seven wheellike Heavens, or levels of reality. Now the Indian texts also inform us that the pillar within the human body, the Rich in Happiness Tree, *is* the Cosmic Tree. When our spiritual energy is at the base of this tree, our consciousness is like that of a serpent or dragon—lustful, greedy, and egocentric. As our energy ascends, life becomes happier and happier until the supreme bliss is realized. To see the Rich in Happiness Tree within the body is to ascend the seven planes of being of the universe, to ascend the Cosmic Tree. Like the seven maidens seated on the wheels of the Cosmic Tree, singing melodious tones, the wheels along the Rich in Happiness Tree are often depicted as seven lotuses, each hymning a single seed syllable. By meditating on the seed syllable, the lotus of its corresponding level opens to an entire realm of being.

The highest point of the Rich in Happiness Tree is the very summit of reality. It is represented by an inverted lotus, a dome of a thousand petals and a thousand syllables, which showers down a thousand streams of spiritual radiance from its position four finger-widths above the top of the skull. Thus to enter this realm, awareness must pass through an invisible hole in the top of the skull. This is an experience of such profundity and universality that it is found widely reflected in archaic architecture and

Ill. 14

cosmology. In the realm of the spirit the human form is identical to the form of the cosmos and the design of dwellings, including not only the Indian temple but also simpler structures such as the Siberian yurt with its smoke hole.

In Siberian cosmology the North Star is a hole in the dome of this world. One passes through it to enter the Highest Heaven. The shaman is able to depart, in spirit, through the hole in the top of his head and enter this Highest Heaven. Thus the shape of the cosmos mirrors this inner experience.

"Up above," gestures a shaman of the Tungus tribe, "there is a certain tree where the souls of the shamans are reared, before they attain their powers. And on the boughs of this tree are nests in which the souls lie and are attended. The name of the tree is 'Turu.' The higher the nest in this tree, the stronger will the shaman be who is raised in it, the more will he know, the farther will he see."[26]

Whenever a young Siberian shaman is initiated, a birch tree is cut and the bark is peeled. On the morning of the rite the tree is erected in the yurt with its roots in the hearth and its top jutting

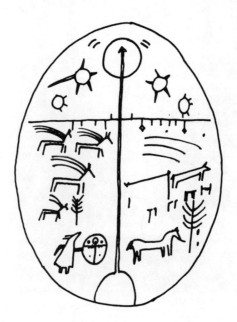

Ill. 15

Ill. 16

up through the smoke hole. The birch is called *udeši-burkhau* or
"guardian of the door"; for on this birch the shaman passes
through the door at the top of the world. This birch is believed
to stand at the center of the world. When the shaman chants the
ancient words and climbs the tree his soul is raised to God, for
the tree grows invisibly during the ascent and extends to the
summit of Heaven. Seven notches cut into the birch represent the
various Heavens along the way. As the shaman climbs, seven bells
sewn onto his costume chime. These symbolize the voices of the
seven celestial maidens that inhabit these Heavens, and at the
very crown of the birch is the smoke hole, representing the Pole
Star, which in turn represents the hole in the top of the head
through which the shaman enters the Highest Heaven. He wears
feathers on his costume and perches atop the birch like a bird, his
head jutting through the smoke hole in the same way as his spirit
juts through the summit of his skull.

When the loftiest of blossoms flowers, the lotus of a thousand petals and a thousand syllables, it is like gaining a new awareness that reaches as far as the dome of the sky, an awareness so vast that it dwarfs one's former state of consciousness. As Emily Dickinson put it: "If I feel physically as if the top of my head were taken off," she proclaimed, "I know this is poetry."

The elegance of Patañjali's expression is evident: he does not advise that we climb a tree or even give a thought to the Rich in Happiness Tree. Yet, as Shear informs us, through meditation on a single, precise formula, the entire reality is revealed. Indian art is as elegant in its representation of this reality as Patañjali. The top of the Cosmic Tree, the essential point from which the entire universe of sound and form issues, is often represented by a dot.

This dot represents the crown *chakra*, the vibratory center presiding over the six lower ones, each with its corresponding level of reality.

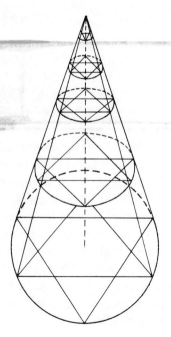

Ill. 17

Ill. 18

When collapsed into a two-dimensional diagram the whole is called the Shri Yantra, a sort of geometry of the spirit.

All the levels of existence are found represented within this simple geometrical figure. When the yogi meditates on the central, still point it vibrates and pulses, expanding to include the inner triangle, the outer triangles, circles, and squares, and finally the mind, body, and surroundings. The lines of the drawing and the forms of the universe resonate like a fine musical instrument plucked with delicate attention. The *yantra* is the visual form of the *mantra,* and just as each level of the Cosmic Tree is associated with a sound, each level of the *yantra* corresponds to a note of the musical scale. The art of music in India is thus based on the universal vibratory centers. And so, as the wisdom of the Vedas, the *mantras* are chanted.

One viewer describes his initial meditation on the *yantra:*

After images of lines become spaces and these spaces as solid ambiguities give off sounds, as if striking taut skins with our open skulls. . . . Eyes follow the outward flow discovering contradictory edges and boundaries breaking. The entire open field becomes an edge, allowing the figures to blossom out and to fold in on the observer. . . . Luckily the image is there to hold on to. One feels the presence of generations of helpful teachers who do not simplify but compress existence into a line, a color, or a dot. The viewer's experiences become the central point. . . . The play-experience of the eye-traced diagrams is the tract that allows the subject-object situation to break down. "Verb-noun" is clarified, and there is a vanishing of "I-that." . . . Viewer and art must blend, allowing the art to look at the observer and empty the room.[27]

As the room is emptied, the human form of the yogi and the humble hut he inhabits open into a thousand-petaled temple. Thus in India, the *yantra,* the shape of the divine cosmos, serves as the blueprint for temples.

For many, the innate structure we are discussing appears not as a tree, but as a mountain with the Pole Star at its summit. The Indian temple, built according to the plan of the *yantra,* is then

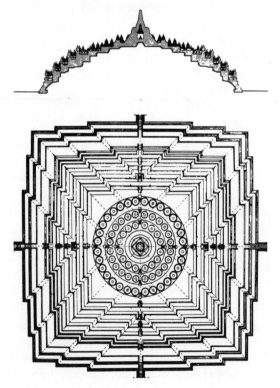

Ill. 19

Ill. 20

a replica of this seven-story mountain, with the Cosmic Axis at its center. The superstructure of such temples forms a cupola, a dome called the *shikhara* or "mountain peak." The word also signifies the peak of sexual bliss, a nipple, and the tuft of hair on the crown of the Buddha's head! This tuft of hair, like the pole situated atop many a temple, represents the crown *chakra*, the vibratory center beyond the top of the head.

Where, then, does this galactic tree-mountain stand? Where is the still center of this turning universe? Are we to bow down several times each day in the direction of the stone in the central city of Mecca as one fifth of the world's population does? Is the Tree of Life in Jerusalem, Rome, or the church down the block? Is the hub of all things in the Japanese temple where a statue of the Buddha sits beneath the Tree of Awakening? Is it in the center of Red Square in Moscow, or at the other central points of our social faiths? Is it in the center of the *yantra?* Or do all these separate, sacred enclosures form one circle without circumference whose center is everywhere and anywhere?

BLACK ELK AT THE CENTER OF THE EARTH

Ill. 21

To answer this question, let us turn to Black Elk, an American Indian medicine man of the Oglala Sioux tribe, who in 1872 had the following vision, as reported by his biographer, John G. Neihardt:

"Then I was standing on the highest mountain of them all, and round about beneath me was the whole hoop of the world. And while I stood there I saw more than I can tell and I understood more than I saw; for I was seeing in a sacred manner the shapes of all things in the spirit, and the shape of all shapes as they must live together like one being. And I saw that the sacred hoop of my people was one of many hoops that made one circle, wide as daylight and as starlight, and in the center grew one mighty flowering tree to shelter all the children of one mother and one father. And I saw that it was holy." Black Elk said that the mountain he stood upon in that vision was Harney Peak in the Black Hills. "But everywhere," he then added, "is the center of the world."[28]

And this is precisely the psychological value of this experience. It is not to replace normal perception with some extraordinary vision. The vision comes spontaneously and allows us to see the center of all things not in our own ego but everywhere. The center of the universe—the point at which the holy enters the profane, eternity merges with time, and infinity stretches out on all sides—is present in every act of attention. Before the dawn of this experience, we are enclosed in a cocoon, a state akin to claustrophobia, hemmed in by the confining illusion of egocentricity. And yet the vision, though unseen, is within us, an immensely powerful, invisible image.

Not knowing it is there we become extremely vulnerable to its external likenesses. We see an image of the sacred center in the environment, and something within us stirs. We become puppets dangling from the fingers of those who are the sacred priests of these images. And within each temple is a holy book, and in each book a holy creed, and in each creed a self-enclosed system and a thousand yes-men to protect it. And somehow the system becomes more important, more holy, than human life, than you and I. The game suddenly becomes terribly, deadly serious, as serious as the somber expressions of those entering a holy shrine. Children don't quite know how to act in such places. They giggle at such a spectacle, and only slowly learn the solemnity of it all—to bow before an image on the central altar before they march off to war, and to lay their pillage before it and praise its glory when, and if, they return. Such bowing down they learn to call humility.

But there are some among us who, though adult, have retained something of the innocence of the child. These are the poets, and they proclaim, like Annie Dillard, that the center is inside ourselves. "I see us all," she says, "as palo santo trees, holy sticks, together watching everything that we watch, and growing in silence." Or there is the Polish master Czeslaw Milosz, who in his *Bells in Winter* writes, "Not that I want to be a god or a hero./Just to change into a tree, grow for ages, not hurt anyone." Poets enter so deeply into the tree of seven stories that they *become* it. They feel the vision blooming within themselves and the entire universe blossoming. Yet the vision is not complete. It is like a child with an ambitious imagination stranded high in the branches, or like the virgins of mythology who become transformed into trees. Though the poet sees the problem more clearly, it takes the vision of a seer to see it fully. Once in a while this happens. Quite unexpectedly from among the generations of worshipers and poets an anomaly appears. Such an anomaly was the nineteenth-century Indian saint Ramakrishna, who one day opened his eyes after meditating and stated flatly, "Some people climb the seven floors of a building and cannot get down; but some climb up and then, at will, visit the lower floors."

Suddenly someone comes to the temple, and instead of placing a wreath of flowers on the figure in the central altar, flings blossoms in a thousand directions. "One day," Ramakrishna reminisced, "it was suddenly revealed to me that everything is Pure Spirit. The utensils of worship, the altar, the door frame—all Pure Spirit. Men, animals, and other living beings—all Pure Spirit. Then like a madman I began to shower flowers in all directions. Whatever I saw I worshiped."[29]

Only a tree in full blossom, a madman, or someone ecstatically in love dances about showering flowers in all directions. In such a life, instead of the human spirit becoming rooted either in the ego or to an external image, the sacred tree has become transformed into a fully human and free being.

As the psychologist Carl Jung discovered, when his patients

Ill. 22

opened to their own inner centers in the process of finding psychic wholeness, transformations took place through symbols that came to them in dreams and visions. Gerhard Adler, a therapist of the Jungian school, tells us of drawings by a forty-nine-year-old woman suffering from claustrophobia that demonstrate just how spontaneously the symbolism of the center may arise.[30] At the beginning of therapy, she saw a persistent vision whenever she shut her eyes. It was of a metal ring held in place by the high tension between four chains stretching off into nothing.

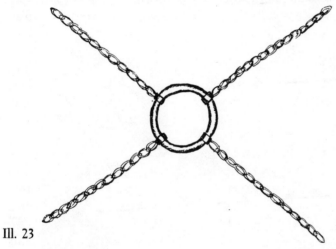

Ill. 23

It is an incomplete image and mirrors her acute state of psychological tension. Nevertheless, the symbol brought the opposing forces of her personality into a sort of focus and acted as a means for the transformation of those forces. In a vague way it looks something like the *yantra* discussed earlier in the chapter; and, in fact, Jung discovered that the internal center that his patients saw in their dreams and visions as they neared psychic wholeness often appeared as a geometrical pattern. The basic design includes a central point, a circle, and some element of fourness, such as a square. In India such designs are called *mandalas*. The vision of the ring seen by Adler's patient contains a circle, but the circle has no center. Furthermore the fourness, the four chains, instead of forming a harmonious whole, leaves an impression of tension, anxiety, and incompleteness.

Over the course of therapy, however, as the opposing forces in her personality came into sharper focus, the images that appeared in her dreams and visions changed.

In her second vision the opposing forces came more fully into view, symbolized by a male and a female, and the central circle became, instead of an iron ring, a jewel. Whereas the accent in the former vision was destructive, here it is constructive. Instead of being pulled apart by four invisible, unknown forces, the two figures are pulled together by rays of energy.

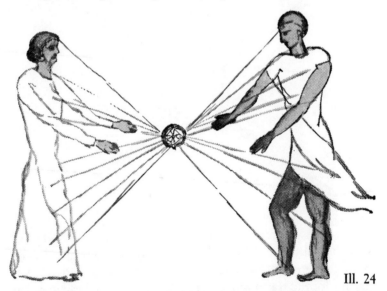

Ill. 24

A further transformation took place in a very powerful vision in which the male and female forces of her personality came into even sharper focus. She called the vision "The Fight With the Angel."

With one of his hands, the angel forced back her head, exposing her breast so that he could hurl a stroke of lightning into her heart. The lightning struck her repeatedly, violently, like a series of electric shocks. She felt that the structures through

Ill. 25

which the electricity coursed were shattered and transformed into a different pattern. She felt that the angel was something quite new, immensely powerful. A numinous inner force penetrated her emotions deeply. The angel was, in fact, the beginning of an eruption of an archetypal image, an image far beyond the realm of the ego, into the realm of the ego. And that is why she felt this as a violent intrusion. The divine was bursting into her consciousness, but her ego tried to hold on and maintain its petty claim on reality.

Her next vision revealed the nature of that archetype. In her encounter with the angel, she found his eyes to be particularly powerful. And she heard what she described as "the music of the spheres" coming from the Pole Star and the stars of the night sky, which she saw constellated about it. The central circle is the Pole Star, but it is also the angel's eye, and what the woman feels to be her true self. Here the opposites are reconciled. No longer is she torn apart by four chains or in the violent embrace of something outside of herself. She has become one with the energy of the angel. Now this painting resembles the Shri Yantra and reminds us of Patañjali's Pole Star *sūtra* in many respects. And as therapy continued, she had an ecstatic realization that the Pole Star and the vast firmament were within herself. At that exact moment her claustrophobia began to be cured.

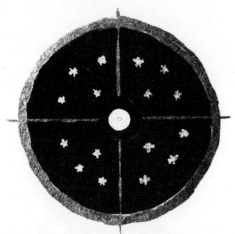

Ill. 26

In the final vision that she painted in the course of therapy, she saw, instead of the tree of our interest, the summit of a mountain, and on it a young man. In the blue firmament shines the solar orb with four prominent golden points, and the central circle is the Angel's eye, the orb of her true self. Just like the birds on top of the pillar in the Indian painting and the feathered young shaman atop his birch, the young man on the summit of the mountain is feathered, free to fly into the infinite firmament and yet in full possession of his individuality.

Ill. 27

The Cosmic Tree, at the Center of the World, then, is ubiquitous. It appears not only in visions, poetry, and architecture, but in art and dreams. Yet, how many of us have truly seen it? After all, it is, as Patañjali says, a *siddhi* or supernatural skill, or, in the words of Wallace Stevens's "A Primitive Like an Orb," "a difficult apperception."

I

The essential poem at the centre of things,
The arias that spiritual fiddlings make,
Have gorged the cast-iron of our lives with good
And the cast-iron of our works. But it is, dear sirs,
A difficult apperception, this gorging good,

Fetched by such slick-eyed nymphs, this essential gold,
This fortune's finding, disposed and re-disposed
By such slight genii in such pale air.

II

We do not prove the existence of the poem.
It is something seen and known in lesser poems.
It is the huge, high harmony that sounds
A little and a little, suddenly,
By means of a separate sense. It is and it
Is not and, therefore, is. In the instant of speech,
The breath of an accelerando moves,
Captivates the being, widens—and was there.

III

What milk there is in such captivity,
What wheaten bread and oaten cake and kind,
Green guests and table in the woods and songs
At heart, within an instant's motion, within
A space grown wide, the inevitable blue
Of secluded thunder, an illusion, as it was,
Oh as, always too heavy for the sense
To seize, the obscurest as, the distant was . . .

IV

One poem proves another and the whole,
For the clairvoyant men that need no proof:
The lover, the believer and the poet.
Their words are chosen out of their desire,
The joy of language, when it is themselves.
With these they celebrate the central poem,
The fulfillment of fulfillments, in opulent,
Last terms, the largest, bulging still with more,

V

Until the used-to earth and sky, and the tree
And cloud, the used-to tree and used-to cloud,
Lose the old uses that they made of them,
And they: these men, and earth and sky, inform

Each other by sharp informations, sharp,
Free knowledges, secreted until then,
Breaches of that which held them fast. It is
As if the central poem became the world,

VI

And the world the central poem, each one the mate
Of the other, as if summer was a spouse,
Espoused each morning, each long afternoon,
And the mate of summer: her mirror and her look,
Her only place and person, a self of her
That speaks, denouncing separate selves, both one.
The essential poem begets the others. The light
Of it is not a light apart, up-hill.

VII

The central poem is the poem of the whole,
The poem of the composition of the whole,
The composition of blue sea and of green,
Of blue light and of green, as lesser poems,
And the miraculous multiplex of lesser poems,
Not merely into a whole, but a poem of
The whole, the essential compact of the parts,
The roundness that pulls tight the final ring

VIII

And that which in an altitude would soar,
A vis, a principle or, it may be,
The meditation of a principle,
Or else an inherent order active to be
Itself, a nature to its natives all
Beneficence, a repose, utmost repose,
The muscles of a magnet aptly felt,
A giant, on the horizon, glistening,

IX

And in bright excellence adorned, crested
With every prodigal, familiar fire,
And unfamiliar escapades: whirroos

And scintillant sizzlings such as children like,
Vested in the serious folds of majesty,
Moving around and behind, a following,
A source of trumpeting seraphs in the eye,
A source of pleasant outbursts on the ear.

X

It is a giant, always, that is evolved,
To be in scale, unless virtue cuts him, snips
Both size and solitude or thinks it does,
As in a signed photograph on a mantelpiece.
But the virtuoso never leaves his shape,
Still on the horizon elongates his cuts,
And still angelic and still plenteous,
Imposes power by the power of his form.

XI

Here, then, is an abstraction given head,
A giant on the horizon, given arms,
A massive body and long legs, stretched out,
A definition with an illustration, not
Too exactly labelled, a large among the smalls
Of it, a close, parental magnitude,
At the centre on the horizon, concentrum, grave
And prodigious person, patron of origins.

XII

That's it. The lover writes, the believer hears,
The poet mumbles and the painter sees,
Each one, his fated eccentricity,
As a part, but part, but tenacious particle,
Of the skeleton of the ether, the total
Of letters, prophecies, perceptions, clods
Of color, the giant of nothingness, each one
And the giant ever changing, living in change.[31]

"Truth," said Heraclitus, "is both willing and unwilling to be called Zeus." The central silence is only silence. Yet it is an order "active to be itself," *active* to become an orderly image.

Thus the vision of the Cosmic Tree blooms. If we are lucky or skilled enough to catch its fragrance, we are blessed. For as it spills its silence all about, it is, as the seers of ancient India advised, the Truth. Yet, as Heraclitus also remarked, "Nature likes to hide." It is "a difficult apperception." And as we move further and further away from the central silence into the din of thoughts and passions, the vision fades, and we each inherit our "fated eccentricity." And so this chapter concludes as it began. Outside my open window dwells an oak. I seldom really see it; I'm too busy. Yet sometimes . . .

Ill. 28

Kên:
Keeping Still, Mountain

In the Celestial Kingdom, which is the name China's ancient monarchs gave their land, words are something like pictures, like a mist that bars one from the clarity of enlightenment. A modern American poet has written of this relationship between words and pictures with insight.

I am trying to describe to you a river at first light.
The water is glassy, under a scud of mist.
It is taking the color of the new sky
but the mist has something else in mind than pink—
a force of discoloration, it would have everything white.
On the far bank are serried low hills, tree-clusters,
occasionally the lights of a car.

This river I want you to see is being remembered.
I tell you this not to make us self-conscious
or conscious of words, but hoping to heighten

the peculiar vividness of a thing imagined.
I put no water-bird or craft on the surface:
the poem is absolutely quiet at about 5 A.M.
Rose-grey water slips away to left and right, silky,
upstream and downstream, just before sunrise,
just before we are called away,
you who don't know me, I who don't know you.

Soon it will be full light. We will blink this river away
and my talking to you, a stranger, as if I knew you,
as if our partaking a strange river at the edge of light
had been no impertinence—this will yield to another subject.
A river talked away, may be the new subject, or,
Mist burned off by the sun, an ancient, common figure,
a nearly dead metaphor, for enlightenment, and
it occurs to me now that someone may have already
accomplished this for you, hundreds of years ago,
someone deft with a brush, in China.[32]

When the Chinese of antiquity established their system of
writing, they did so according to the following tacit rule: simply
draw a picture to represent a thing or idea. Such a picture, like
William Meredith's poem about the pictorial nature of language,
is called an ideogram, an idea made graphic. To write "tree" in
Chinese, you take hold of the bamboo handle of a brush, dip it
in black ink, and then execute what is essentially a painting, an
ideogram of a tree:

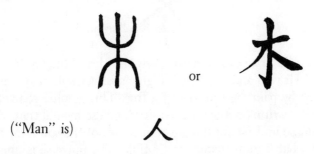

or

("Man" is)

If you want to write "forest" or "grove," again you must produce a painting—and this time something of a landscape:

The ideogram for "sun" is

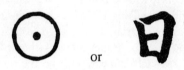

or

When this is joined to the ideogram for "tree," it becomes something a little more abstract:

the sun in a tree, hence "east." And the root (of a tree) means something even more abstract:

"origin."

Now the idea of an origin, particularly the idea of the mysterious origin of Heaven and Earth, is a highly abstract notion. Yet it is conveyed by painting the root of a tree. This graphic character of Chinese writing betrays a pervasive Chinese mental trait. For the Chinese understand things, even things of the spirit, on the basis of what is immediately perceptible. The universe is simply *shan, ho, ta-ti,* "mountains, rivers, and the great Earth." A wandering monk is *yun-shui,* "clouds and water" (sex is "clouds and rain"), and a monastic community is *ts'ung-lin*, "a peaceful grove where trees and grasses grow together in harmony."

The young Mao Tse-tung encountered this Chinese proclivity to treat spiritual matters in terms of minute particulars just after he graduated from college and was wandering on foot with a friend through the Chinese countryside. One evening the pair came upon a Buddhist monastery and decided to see if they could get a meal. They knocked, and a monk appeared. Young Mao stated that they had not come to worship the Buddha, but would simply like some food. To his astonishment, the monk replied that there is no difference between eating and worshiping the Buddha, and welcomed them in. Partaking of a simple bowl of rice, among those who grow together as peacefully as trees and grasses in a grove, becomes a way of harmonizing the whole universe or, I should say, a way of harmonizing mountains, rivers, and the great Earth.

If you were a sage in very ancient China, in order to know the future all you would need to do was consult a tortoise shell. For the shell of the tortoise, like an Indian temple, was thought to be shaped like the universe. The upper, domed part seemed like the vault of Heaven, and the lower, square section like the four directions of Earth. You merely placed the shell in a fire, and when it cracked the pattern of the fissures indicated the opinion of the Gods on sacrifice, hunting, fishing, weather, illness, and healing. Something of this tradition survives in the form of the fortune cookie.

Yarrow is a weed native to Eurasia. It is found today, however, in California, where it grows along roadsides, recognizable by its flat clusters of white flowers set atop long woody stalks, which wave in the airstreams of vehicles passing by at fifty-five miles per hour. During the sixties, oil being more plentiful, the vehicles passed at an even greater pace, the yarrow waved even more vigorously, and it was even harvested by hippies given to orientalism.

It seems that thousands of years ago divination by means of tortoise shells suddenly gave way to divination by means of yarrow stalks. Of course in that distant era they were not used to divine whether one should hitch to San Francisco to see the Stones or to New York to catch Dylan. The yarrow stalks were used in conjunction with an encyclopedia of oracles called *The Book of Changes (I Ching)*. It is an obscure book, consisting of a series of symbols—diagrams of hard, solid (——) and soft, broken (– –) lines. These represent the two major principles in Chinese culture, *yang* and *yin*, respectively. In writing, *yang* is represented by the ideogram for the sun's rays. Thus *yang* is all that is bright, dry, warm, hard, masculine, round, odd-numbered, and upward moving. *Yin* is represented by the ideogram for a rain cloud. Thus *yin* is all that is dark, wet, cold, soft, female, square, even-numbered, and downward moving. The shady side of a mountain, tree, or street is its *yin* side. Cross the street into the sun, and *yang* predominates. Everything is composed of *yin* and *yang* qualities. As the universe—mountains, rivers, and the great Earth—is always in a state of flux, *yin* and *yang* are continually, and cyclically, changing. And yet there is something that transcends this ebb and flow of light and shadow. It is called the Tao, the Way, or the Great Extreme.

How, then, did the universe—the mountains, rivers, and great Earth—come to be? The Great Extreme, it is said, gave birth to the two Primal Forms, like two kinds of fissures on a cracked tortoise shell:

The Two Primal Forms gave birth to the Four Symbols, which consist of all the possible combinations of pairs that can be formed from the Primal Pair:

These mated to produce the Eight Trigrams:

Ch'ien, the Creative, strong, Heaven, father

▰▰ K'un, the Receptive, devoted, yielding, Earth, mother

▰▰ Chên, the Arousing, inciting movement, Thunder, first son

▰▰ K'an, the Abysmal, dangerous, Water, second son

▰▰ Kên, Keeping Still, repose, Mountain, third son

▰▰ Sun, the Gentle, penetrating, Wind, Wood, first daughter

▰▰ Li, the Clinging, light giving, Fire, second daughter

▰▰ Tui, the Joyous, joyful, Lake, third daughter

From the Eight Trigrams the Sixty-four Hexagrams were produced. These represent the entire interplay of *yin* and *yang* in space and time, and how we pass from one transformation of reality to another. In the circular arrangement of the hexagrams, Heaven is above, symbolized by six *yang* lines: ▰▰ Earth is below, symbolized by six *yin* lines: ▰▰

Night and day, the play of the seasons and of sexual love, the coming and going of the breath, the appearance and disappearance of the spirit, indeed the whole cosmos pulses between Heaven and Earth, *yin* and *yang*.

When one casts the yarrow stalks, the great Tao dictates a line, either solid or broken. When six lines have been determined in this way, a hexagram is thus formed that is the precise expres-

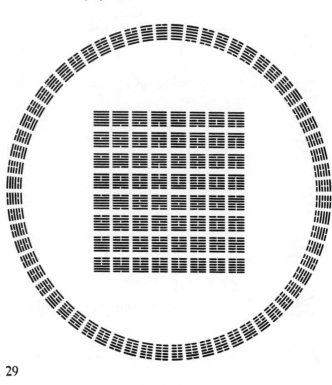

Ill. 29

sion of *yin* and *yang* at that time and place. It is then merely a matter of finding the corresponding hexagram in *The Book of Changes* and applying the oracle to one's own case, whether it be solving a pressing problem or merely clarifying a vague intuition. The text of the oracle accompanying each hexagram is so obscure, and the images contained in the oracle are so archetypal, that they form suitable objects for meditation. Like the Vedic riddles, the oracles can be used as mental tools to evoke an intuitive response.

If the yarrow stalks should fall in just the right manner, we would obtain the following hexagram with its oracle:

It is called 艮 , Kên, Keeping Still, Mountain. And that's it. Keeping Still, Mountain.

Now this is precisely the same, abiding image as that found in Patañjali's Pole Star *sūtra*. It is the immovable Cosmic Axis, whether it be tree, mountain, or merely that stillness of thought which is reflected in these. The oracle appended to this image reads:

KEEPING STILL. Keeping his back still
So that he no longer feels his body.
He goes into his courtyard
And does not see his people.
No blame.[33]

Ill. 30

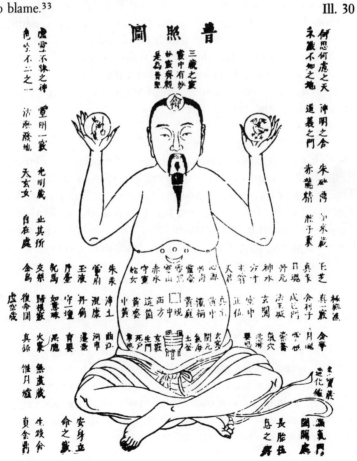

Just as in India, the backbone *is* the Cosmic Axis with its seven ascending vibratory centers; here each of the six lines in the hexagram becomes a plateau of spiritual energy in the body of the Chinese sage. The text on the bottom line of Kên advises stillness in the toes. The next line calls for stillness in the calves. The next, stillness in the hips; and so on to the trunk, the jaw, and finally the top line calling for Noblehearted Keeping Still. In this way, the body of the Chinese sage becomes totally still, so that he no longer feels his body, which *becomes* Keeping Still, Mountain. And what happens when we meditate on the still, the abiding star or mountain? As we learned in the previous chapter, meditation on the still is the climate in which the Cosmic Tree blooms. It is no surprise, then, that the very next hexagram in *The Book of Changes* after Kên, Keeping Still, Mountain, is Sun; composed of the trigram Kên, Keeping Still, Mountain, on top of which towers a tree, the gentle, Wood.

This hexagram represents the idea of gradual development, through the image of a tree growing gently on a still mountain. The tree is in no hurry; it grows inch by inch, firmly rooted, and according to the laws of its own being. Just as the Indian Cosmic Tree is inhabited by birds symbolizing the ascent of the spirit to the highest realm, and as the Siberian shaman climbs the birch in the rite of initiation, the text on this hexagram speaks of a wild goose, the Chinese symbol of the spirit, which flies to the summit of the mountain, then to the crown of the tree, and finally, like the spirit of the yogi and the shaman, disappears into Heaven.

In the eternal romance between *yang* and *yin,* the Chinese universe is not all still mountains rising into Heaven. It is also flowing rivers and the great Earth. *Yang* and *yin* are in continual flux. And so, as a final, graceful touch, the text informs us that when the wild goose vanishes into Heaven, the ultimate *yang,* his feathers float down to the great Earth, the ultimate *yin,* where they are used in the sacred dances in the temples.

Ill. 31

Ill. 32

Yak

All men know the use of the useful, but nobody knows the use of the useless.

Where can I find a man who has forgotten words so that I can have a word with him?

—CHUANG TZU

Taoism is the primordial and true Way in China. I do not call it a religion, for there is no word for religion in the Celestial Kingdom. The Chinese merely call the highest good the Way, the Tao. Above all, the Way is natural, delighting in the spontaneous and unpretentious. Taoists seek, through meditation, to surrender to this transcendent, changeless power at the basis of all change. Tao harmonizes and maintains life. The endless expanses of mountains, rivers, rain and clouds, Heaven and Earth, man and woman, emperor and subjects follow the Tao. The more they follow it, the more their lives are spontaneous, harmonious, and natural—devoid of all that is controlled or restricted.

The great Taoist sages often adopted a rural way of life or took refuge in the most inaccessible regions of rivers and mountains, living the lives of simple fishermen. These true purists dwelt among the remotest mountains, far from the hustle and bustle of civilization and the influence of princes. They sought such deep

seclusion because they were in such great demand. For to have
the beneficent presence of a Taoist holy man in one's court was
to be ensured a harmonious and long rule. It was not that the sage
had to do anything in particular; he was valuable chiefly because
of the depth of his nondoing, his unseen spiritual influence. At
the very most, a sage might be asked to administer a region, or
to give advice, much in the manner that a ruler would consult a
tortoise shell or *The Book of Changes* for an oracle. But the sages
shunned all such activities and instead praised the usefulness of
uselessness.

Sometimes a great Taoist would openly ridicule a prince and
the prince's futile attempts to bring about law and order through
force. According to Chuang Tzu, one of the most vocal Taoist
masters, the only way to get rid of an annoying sage was to offer
him the throne! This would insult the sage so deeply that he
would more than likely jump into the nearest river holding a rock!

Ill. 33

"Once, when Chuang Tzu was fishing in the P'u River, the king of Ch'u sent two officials to go and announce to him: 'I would like to trouble you with the administration of my realm.'

"Chuang Tzu held on to the fishing pole and, without turning his head, said, 'I have heard that there is a sacred tortoise in Ch'u that has been dead for three thousand years. The king keeps it wrapped in cloth and boxed, and stores it in the ancestral temple. Now would this tortoise rather be dead and have its bones left behind and honored? Or would it rather be alive and dragging its tail in the mud?'

" 'It would rather be alive and dragging its tail in the mud,' said the two officials.

"Chuang Tzu said, 'Go away! I'll drag my tail in the mud!' "³⁴

There are other Taoist tales regarding the value of uselessness. Most often they deal with trees. In the Celestial Kingdom shrines were always located in groves of stately trees, which lent the sacred places special sanctity. One day "Carpenter Shih went to Ch'i and, when he got to Crooked Shaft, he saw a serrate oak standing by the village shrine. It was broad enough to shelter several thousand oxen and measured a hundred spans around, towering above the hills. The lowest branches were eighty feet from the ground, and a dozen or so of them could have been made into boats. There were so many sightseers that the place looked like a fair, but the carpenter didn't even glance around and went on his way without stopping. His apprentice stood staring for a long time and then ran after Carpenter Shih and said, 'Since I first took up my ax and followed you, Master, I have never seen timber as beautiful as this. But you don't even bother to look, and go right on without stopping. Why is that?'

" 'Forget it—say no more!' said the carpenter. 'It's a worthless tree! Make boats of it and they'd sink; make coffins and they'd rot in no time; make vessels and they'd break at once. Use it for doors and it would sweat like pine; use it for posts and the worms would eat them up. It's not a timber tree—there's nothing it can be used for. That's how it got to be that old!'

"After Carpenter Shih had returned home, the oak tree appeared to him in a dream and said, 'What are you comparing me with? Are you comparing me with those useful trees? The cherry apple, the pear, the orange, the citron, the rest of those fructiferous trees and shrubs—as soon as their fruit is ripe, they are torn apart and subjected to abuse. Their big limbs are broken off, their little limbs are yanked around. Their utility makes life miserable for them, and so they don't get to finish out the years Heaven gave them, but are cut off in mid-journey. They bring it on themselves—the pulling and tearing of the common mob. And it's the same with all other things.

" 'As for me, I've been trying a long time to be of no use, and though I almost died, I've finally got it. This is of great use to me. If I had been of some use, would I ever have grown this large? Moreover you and I are both of us things. What's the point of this—things condemning things? You, a worthless man about to die—how do you know I'm a worthless tree?'

"When Carpenter Shih woke up, he reported his dream. His apprentice said, 'If it's so intent on being of no use, what's it doing there at the village shrine?' 'Shhh! Say no more! It's only *resting* there. If we carp and criticize, it will merely conclude that we don't understand it. Even if it weren't at the shrine, do you suppose it would be cut down? It protects itself in a different way from ordinary people. If you try to judge it by conventional standards, you'll be way off!' "[35]

The oak abides because it is useless. "All men know the use of the useful," says Chuang Tzu, "but nobody knows the use of the useless."[36] And as it is with the useless Tao, holy men, and trees, so it is with useless words.

"Hui Tzu said to Chuang Tzu, 'I have a big tree of the kind men call *shu*. Its trunk is too gnarled and bumpy to apply a measuring line to, its branches too bent and twisty to match up to a compass or a square. You could stand it by the road and no carpenter would look at it twice. Your words, too, are big and useless, and so everyone alike spurns them!'

"Chuang Tzu said, 'Maybe you've never seen a wildcat or a

weasel. It crouches down and hides, watching for something to come along. It leaps and races east and west, not hesitating to go high or low—until it falls into the trap and dies in the net. Then again there's the yak, big as a cloud covering the sky. It certainly knows how to be big, though it doesn't know how to catch rats. Now you have this big tree and you're distressed because it's useless. Why don't you plant it in Not-Even-Anything Village, or the field of Broad-and-Boundless, relax and do nothing by its side, or lie down for a free and easy sleep under it? Axes will never shorten its life, nothing can ever harm it. If there's no use for it, how can it come to grief or pain?' "[37]

Chuang Tzu's words, like the gnarled and bumpy tree, are useless. There are no conventional standards to apply to them. They are immeasurable. It is as though they are planted in the field of Broad-and-Boundless. In his reply, though Chuang Tzu speaks about a weasel, a cloud, a yak, and a tree, he is really explaining the use of useless words. Language becomes really useful when it is as if planted in Not-Even-Anything Village, when it is rooted in infinity and one relaxes and does nothing by its side. Mere words and concepts are like the net in which the mind, like the wildcat, gets caught. Chuang Tzu, however, uses words like a crowbar, to humorously pry loose the trap or tear the net. He is not above using offensive language if it will clear the cobwebs and concepts from the head of an especially dull listener. When asked where the Tao is to be found, he once replied,

" 'There's no place it doesn't exist.'

" 'Come,' said Master Tung-kuo, 'you must be more specific!'

" 'It is in the ant.'

" 'As low a thing as that?'

" 'It is in the panic grass.'

" 'But that's lower still!'

" 'It is in the tiles and shards.'

" 'How can it be so low?'

" 'It is in the piss and shit.' "[38]

We have all read language that refers to the oneness of all

things. This book, for instance, is full of it. I have, however, attempted to show the limits of such language, as Chuang Tzu does in the following passage, which pokes fun at the silliness of much philosophical thought:

"Now I am going to make a statement here. I don't know whether it fits into the category of other people's statements or not. But whether it fits into their category or whether it doesn't, it obviously fits into some category. So in that respect it is no different from their statements. However, let me try making my statement.

"There is a beginning. There is a not yet beginning to be a beginning. There is a not yet beginning to be a not yet beginning to be a beginning. There is being. There is nonbeing. There is a not yet beginning to be nonbeing. There is a not yet beginning to be a not yet beginning to be nonbeing. Suddenly there is nonbeing. But I do not know, when it comes to nonbeing, which is really being and which is nonbeing. Now I have just said something. But I don't know whether what I have said has really said something or whether it hasn't said something.

"There is nothing in the world bigger than the tip of an autumn hair, and Mount T'ai is tiny. No one has lived longer than a dead child, and P'eng-tsu died young. Heaven and earth were born at the same time I was, and the ten thousand things are one with me.

"We have already become one, so how can I say anything? But I have just *said* that we are one, so how can I not be saying something? The one and what I said about it make two, and two and the original one make three. If we go on this way, then even the cleverest mathematician can't tell where we'll end, much less an ordinary man. If by moving from nonbeing to being we get to three, how far will we get if we move from being to being? Better not to move, but to let things be!

"The Way has never known boundaries; speech has no constancy. But because of [the recognition of a] 'this,' there came to be boundaries. Let me tell you what the boundaries are. There is left, there is right, there are theories, there are debates, there are divisions, there are discriminations, there are emulations, and there are contentions. These are called the Eight Virtues. As to what is beyond the Six Realms, the sage admits its existence but does not theorize. As to what is within the Six Realms, he theorizes, but does not debate. In the case of the *Spring and Autumn*, the record of the former kings of past ages, the sage debates but does not discriminate. So [I say,] those who divide fail to divide; those who discriminate fail to discriminate. What does this mean, you ask? The sage embraces things. Ordinary men discriminate among them and parade their discriminations before others. So I say, those who discriminate fail to see."[39]

Chuang Tzu doesn't present us with theories; he plays with language in a nonsensical way in order to demonstrate that many of the ways that we use language seriously are equally nonsensical. And "the importance of nonsense," observes Gary Zukav in *The Dancing Wu Li Masters*, "hardly can be overstated. The more clearly we experience something as 'nonsense,' the more clearly we are experiencing the boundaries of our own self-imposed cognitive structures. 'Nonsense' is that which does not fit into the prearranged patterns which we have superimposed on reality. There is no such thing as 'nonsense' apart from a judgemental intellect which calls it that."[40] Chuang Tzu attempts to show us that the attempt to talk about metaphysical things in the guise of ordinary language results in nonsense. And through the intentional use of nonsense, he hopes to *show* us what metaphysics can only *talk* about, by removing the cobwebs of words from our eyes. He realizes that he cannot escape from words, that he is playing a language-game, but he *recognizes* that he is, and takes the game to its extreme limit.

Just as kings and princes would journey to the most remote wastes of their realms to ask the advice of Taoist hermits, the discursive mind tries to grasp the ineffable with words and concepts. Chuang Tzu tells us of the mind's journey to its most remote and silent provinces:

"Knowledge wandered north to the banks of the Black Waters, climed the Knoll of Hidden Heights, and there by chance came upon Do-Nothing-Say-Nothing. Knowledge said to Do-Nothing-Say-Nothing, 'There are some things I'd like to ask you. What sort of pondering, what sort of cognition does it take to know the Way? What sort of surroundings, what sort of practices does it take to find rest in the Way? What sort of path, what sort of procedure will get me to the Way?'

"Three questions he asked, but Do-Nothing-Say-Nothing didn't answer. It wasn't that he just didn't answer—he didn't know *how* to answer!

"Knowledge, failing to get any answer, returned to the White Waters of the south, climbed the summit of Dubiety Dismissed, and there caught sight of Wild-and-Witless. 'Ah—I know!' said Wild-and-Witless. 'And I'm going to tell you.' But just as he was about to say something, he forgot what it was he was about to say.

"Knowledge, failing to get any answer, returned to the imperial palace, where he was received in audience by the Yellow Emperor, and posed his questions. The Yellow Emperor said, 'Only when there is no pondering and no cogitation will you get to know the Way. Only when you have no surroundings and follow no practices will you find rest in the Way. Only when there is no path and no procedure can you get to the Way.'

"Knowledge said to the Yellow Emperor, 'You and I know, but those other two that I asked didn't know. Which of us is right, I wonder?'

"The Yellow Emperor said, 'Do-Nothing-Say-Nothing—he's the one who is truly right. Wild-and-Witless appears to be so. But you and I in the end are nowhere near it. Those who know do not speak; those who speak do not know. Therefore the sage practices the teaching that has no words.' "41

Gone are all the useful words of Chuang Tzu's more practical-minded contemporaries. Yet Chuang Tzu's useless nonsense, twenty-five hundred years old, endures like the useless oak because it reveals, however imperfectly, that which abides beyond mere concepts and words. The paradox is that Chuang Tzu's useless words sound at times very much like the expressions of our very practical-minded modern physicists. When the New Physics came into being with the revolutionary concept of a field, physicists met up with a view of reality that, when described in ordinary language, came out sounding very much like another legendary Taoist sage, Lao Tzu. For instance, in his *Essay in Physics*, Herbert Samuel suggests that energy exists in two states simultaneously—quiescent and active—and flows effortlessly from one state to the next.

Quiescent energy is conceived as a continuum, and as the sole physical constituent of the universe. All material events are to be accounted for as cases of the activation of quiescent energy.

Being quiescent it is undifferentiated, and produces no phenomena. It cannot therefore be perceived, or defined, or described, and nothing can be located or timed by reference to it.

It does not follow from this that it is non-existent. Its existence is demonstrated by the emergence and behavior of active energy. It is one of those unobservables whose reality is inferred from the phenomena that have been observed.[42]

Compare this with the opening passage of Lao Tzu's famous work, *The Way and Its Power.*

The Tao (Way) that can be grasped by the concept "Tao"
    Is not the limitless Tao;
The name that can be named
    Is not the limitless name.
The state in which there are no names and concepts
    Is the origin of Heaven and Earth;
The state in which there are names and concepts
    Is the mother of all things.

Always beyond concepts,
    That we may intuit its backgroundness;
Always in the realm of conceptual desire,
    That we may discern its manifestations.
These two are the same;
    Yet they receive different names.

That they are the same is the mystery.

Mystery of all mysteries!
The door of all subtleties![43]

Both the scientist and the sage speak of an immense reservoir of pure creative potentiality transcending all conceptualization. Though this field is the sole constituent of the universe, it gives rise to distinctions and material bodies, which are just fluctuations of it. Both scientist and sage realize that language, with its concepts and distinctions, keeps us from being aware of undifferentiated wholeness. Only the sage, however, is able to overcome language, gain immediate experience of this field, and put it to use for the good of all creatures.

We are already familiar with the Indian concept of Dharma, the silent force that upholds all the laws of activity in nature and in human conduct; and we have seen that the yogi needs only to attune himself to this force through meditation in order to act harmoniously. Though Dharma is silent and inactive, it is the basis of all right action. The yogi attuned to Dharma is filled with this deep silence to such a degree that silence coexists with activity. Inactive Dharma coexists with all activity. Thus the Indian scriptures say that the wise see nonaction in action, and action in nonaction. The nonactive aspect of activity is that which lies at its very basis, guiding and supporting actions so that they are in accordance with universal law.

It was much the same with the Chinese sages. In the Celestial Kingdom there were two major schools of thought concerning how to behave in the best manner. On the one hand there were the Confucianists. They felt that to act in accordance with Heaven one must sincerely follow all the rules of Propriety that apply to one's station in life. If you are a ruler, you follow the rules of Propriety applicable to that station. If you are a servant, you follow another set of rules. One can imagine how the Confucianists felt about the Taoists, who didn't give the least bit of attention to rules and regulations. They simply sought the immensity of the Tao and then behaved spontaneously.

A story illustrates the difference between the two schools: a Taoist master was sitting naked in his mountain cabin meditating.

Meanwhile a group of Confucianist do-gooders entered the door of this hut, having hiked up the mountain from the village to lecture him on the rules of proper conduct. Naturally, when they saw the sage sitting naked before them, they were shocked and asked, "What are you doing, sitting in your hut without any pants on?" The sage replied, "This entire universe is my hut. This little hut is my pants. What are you fellows doing inside my pants?"

Like the oak, the Taoist masters were perfectly natural. They sought to be like the oak and like the Tao, which, as Lao Tzu says, never does anything and yet never leaves anything undone. The oak, abiding in its own simple nature, is filled with the Tao and endures. Neither does the sage act; it is the power of the Tao that acts through him whether he is overtly active or inactive. He simply becomes like a leaf riding the wind of the Tao, unable to tell if he is carrying the wind along or the wind is carrying him. Any individual effort obstructs the flow of this infinite potency. Through such power the mere presence of the sage is enough to ensure harmony and prosperity in an entire region. Whenever a sage did offer advice on how to rule a kingdom, he would invariably say that all the king needed to do was seek the Tao and all would be well. As Lao Tzu said, you can govern an entire kingdom without leaving your room.

For all their seeming passivity and reclusiveness, the Taoists were not irresponsible. They were deeply concerned with a profound art of government and endowed with a power over events undreamed of by worldly men. Through their immersion in this power, the great ancestral monarchs and sage-kings of the Celestial Kingdom's golden age ruled without ruling and created order without giving orders.

六
騎牛
歸家

Ill. 34

Mu

Student: What is the meaning of Zen?
Master: The oak tree in the courtyard.

—Zen dialogue

KOAN

For the Buddhist, language is *theoretically* neither loving nor lovable and possesses neither divinity nor revelatory power. It is simply an illusory force binding us to our distorted view of reality. Yet in *practice* the Buddhist points this out to us by means of language. Thus while in theory Buddhists find language somewhat distasteful, in practice they neither adore nor disgustedly abandon words; they lock horns with them.

Zen Buddhism was deeply influenced by Chinese Taoism, whose venerable sages distrusted, yet ultimately yielded to, the necessity of speech. "Show me a man who has forgotten words," proclaimed Chuang Tzu, "so that I may have a word with him." And Chuang Tzu, like the Indians with their use of *mantras*, used seemingly useless words to battle, chide, and demolish the trap of conceptual thought.

Now Zen is a tradition that claims to be beyond all scriptures, independent of words and letters—a tradition pointing directly to the human mind, seeing into its own nature and attaining Buddhahood. Yet, for all this talk about freedom from words, letters, and scriptures, this is a tradition in which language is of supreme importance. For it is *within* and *through language* that the human mind points to itself and that is done, as we have said, by locking horns with language, especially through the Zen riddle or *koan*.

These riddles arose in the day-to-day monastic life of ancient Zen communities. The very earliest Zen teachers realized that the real gristle of Buddhism was not to be found in volumes of philosophical ponderings or in lofty scriptures, but in the psychology of individuals in day-to-day life. In their mountain monasteries, the early masters lived in intimate contact with their students. While working together in the garden, preparing meals, and eating, the students would come up with questions having to do with the immediate situation or more often some abstract, philosophical problem. Often with no more than a short phrase, or even a single word, the master would bring them to a deeper level of realization. Many times the teacher would ask another question in reply. Eventually these questions, replies, and riddles were collected, and they are used to this day in Zen.

"What is the color of the number three?" "Can a machine have a toothache?" "How can you hang a thief who doesn't exist?" "Do we think with our feet?" These questions were posed in order to baffle, insult, cajole, or kick our minds into a clearer perception of language and thus reality. They are not Zen riddles, however, but problems devised by a Western philosopher named Ludwig Wittgenstein, whose method of doing philosophy has often been compared to the methods of Zen.

Many students of philosophy, upon encountering Wittgenstein, drop out of school and take up the study of Zen. Yet about an equal number of Zen students, hearing of Wittgenstein, drop out of the monastery and start doing philosophy. Both Zen and

Wittgenstein use nonsense intentionally, in the same way as Chuang Tzu used his useless words.

In his early years Wittgenstein divided language into sense and nonsense. Language that makes sense is simply language that states facts about the world of the senses. Yet he found that language has a tendency toward nonsense. Library shelves, after all, are full of books discussing how many angels can fit on the head of a pin, and other such weighty matters. Language tends to drift toward its own limits, trying to say what is really beyond words. We "thrust against the limits of language," says Wittgenstein, "but the tendency, the thrust *points to something*. . . . I can only say I don't belittle this human tendency; I take my hat off to it."[44]

As Chuang Tzu pointed out, this proclivity of language to talk about things it cannot really talk about is especially apparent in the subjects of philosophy and religion. Wittgenstein admits that his whole tendency

and I believe the tendency of all men who ever tried to write or talk Ethics or Religion was to run against the boundaries of language. This running against the walls of our language is perfectly, absolutely hopeless. Ethics, so far as it springs from the desire to say something about the ultimate meaning of life, the absolute good, the absolute value, can be no science. What it says does not add to our knowledge in any sense. But it is a document of a tendency in the human mind which I personally cannot help respecting deeply and I would not for my life ridicule it.[45]

We constantly try to twist and contort language into doing what it was not really meant to do. We talk about "love," "faith," and "God"—and yet these words have no definite meaning. Everyone uses them differently. If everyone knew *the* meaning of the word "God," why would thousands of volumes be devoted to the arguments of theologians? Why would Protestants and Catholics be at war in Ireland? It seems that we can only converse with someone who uses words in the same way we do. If someone plays the same game with the sound "God" as we do, then we are able to play along. Wittgenstein realized that it is useless to search for

the meaning of a word. He said that the meaning of a word is in its use. We choose the meaning a word will have by the way we use it. A community forms around words that are used in the same way by other members of the community.

At this point a problem arises. If the meaning of every word depends upon its use, if each word is diverse in its application, what is the best method of showing this? Wittgenstein felt that one could not overcome the bewitchment of language by sitting and listening to lectures or reading books. Just like the Zen masters who directly confronted the deep questions of their students, Wittgenstein felt philosophy has something profoundly personal about it, something that requires attentive discussion.

The method of discussion Wittgenstein used to convey his insights into language was what he called language-games. These games played within language reveal that we are bound up in words and that words are used in quite diverse ways. So when he asks, "What color is the number three?" or, "Can a machine have a toothache?" he forces us to bump our heads up against language, to lock horns with it in such a way that we see words as we never have before—eye to eye. By really seeing language clearly we realize the limits of language and that many of our philosophical and religious perplexities have more to do with language than with truth or God. The aim of this method is not to *solve* philosophical and religious perplexities but to *dissolve* them by demonstrating their linguisticality and absurdity. Philosophical perplexities are seen as queer illnesses—"they are deep disquietudes; their roots are as deep in us as the forms of our language."[46] Wittgenstein's queer questions help us see that many of our own questions are equally strange, that many of them have the form (to quote a famous Buddhist example): "Is the hair of a tortoise smooth or hard?"

Wittgenstein realized that it is mainly when language goes on vacation, or on a holiday—when it is used philosophically or religiously—that questions of meaning arise. After all, we seldom inquire what someone means when we are asked to wash the dishes, or to look at the oak tree in the courtyard. And this is wh

when the Zen master is asked the meaning of Zen, he directs our attention to some dirty dishes and a tub of water, or to an oak tree. We think that "Zen," like any other word, must have some *object* that corresponds to it and that is apart from dirty dishes and oak trees. But it is only a trick of language. There is no such *thing* as *Zen*, other than dirty dishes and oak trees. It is like trying to find *length*. A stick does not exist without length, but length is not a *thing*. Yet we use it in sentences that make it sound as if it is a thing. We say, "A stick has length," just as we say, "A cow has ears."

Like Wittgenstein, Zen uses intentional nonsense to cut through conceptions born of language. Rather than build up a logical system of concepts in which definite answers can be given to definite problems, Zen attempts to transcend logic and systems. Just as Wittgenstein thought of philosophical disquietude as a kind of illness, a Zen saying proclaims that the desire

To know the original Mind, the essential Nature,
This is the great disease of Zen.

One day, wishing to know his essential nature, a student approached the famous Zen teacher Joshu and spoke: "A single light is divided into millions of lights; what then is the origin of this single light?" A philosopher could write an entire book on this problem, but Joshu, abandoning words, simply tossed off one of his shoes, in effect answering that the question and not his answer contained the nonsense.

Whereas many religions make a sharp distinction between the serious business of spirituality and humor, in Zen it has become something of a tradition to laugh. Wittgenstein once said that he could imagine a religion composed entirely of jokes—and it seems at times that Zen is like a joke that you either get or don't. If fact, Zen masters often clown around so much that their behavior seems almost idiotic. They are something of a mixture of nitwit, madman, trickster, jester, and clown. Reading of the antics and teachings of these characters often leaves the impression of a sort of Zen circus.

Consider Seppō, who always kept three wooden balls with him. Whenever anyone approached him wanting to know the meaning of Zen he would just juggle the balls and roll them about like some bear in a circus. Then there is Sekitō, who repelled philosophical inquiries with a curt "Shut up! Don't bark like a dog, please!" Or consider Tenryū, who, when asked by his student Gutei about the path to enlightenment, simply held up his finger. And at that very instant, Gutei was enlightened.

And so it happened that Gutei himself became a Zen master. Whenever he was asked a particularly thorny question concerning Zen, he would raise his finger, but always at the least expected moment. The man was like living lightning. When his students saw him, they knew that the thunder could come at any instant. But he always held up that finger when they were least prepared. One day a student started imitating this finger-raising Zen. When Gutei learned of these antics, he grasped the student and cut off his finger with a knife! The student ran away crying. Gutei shouted, and when the student stopped and turned his head, Gutei raised his own finger. In that very instant the thunder roared for the student, and never stopped.

Then there was the master Teng Yin Fong, who was just about to die. He said to those gathered by his bedside that he had seen monks die while lying down and even while sitting, but wanted to know if any had died while standing. His friends said that yes, some monks had died standing. "How about upside down?" asked the master, who then stood on his head and died. Such humor, even in the face of death, demonstrates that these were not simply clowns, but men who had achieved a high degree of spiritual freedom.

One of the axioms of Buddhism is that all things have the Buddha-nature, and one *koan* concerns the student who asked Joshu whether a dog has the Buddha-nature. Joshu simply shouted, "Mu!" If we were to look it up in a Japanese dictionary we would learn that "Mu" means "no" or "nothing."

This became one of the most famous *koans* of all. Yatsutami, a modern Zen teacher, assigned Mu to a student, explaining that literally the expression means "no" or "not," but the significance of Joshu's answer does not lie in this. *Mu* is the expression of the living, functioning, dynamic Buddha-nature. What you must do is discover the spirit or essence of this *Mu,* not through intellectual analysis but by searching into your innermost being. Then you must demonstrate before me, concretely and vividly, that you understand *Mu* as living truth, without recourse to conceptions, or abstract explanations. Remember, you can't understand *Mu* through ordinary cognition, you must grasp it directly with your whole being.[47]

After being assigned a period of intense meditation on Mu, a student may be interviewed by the teacher, who will insist, "How much does Mu weigh?" "How old is Mu?" "Show me Mu!" The student may hesitate, or give a premeditated or abstract philosophical response. This will only end in the teacher telling the student to enter into Mu even more deeply, or the student may be told that Mu is the only barrier to enlightenment.

After further practice the student may suddenly have the experience of seeing Mu everywhere: in a bowl of rice, the path through the garden, a frog leaping into the pond, the trees, the sky . . . Everything, even the simple act of scratching one's arm, becomes nothing but Mu. This comes not as an intellectual realization, but as an overwhelming experience in which each object seems radiantly alive in its own being. Mu has deepened and gloriously enlivened perception, breaking down the bewitchment of language and its concepts. What "useful" language has given— concepts and confusion—"useless" language removes.

Thus it is with language that the heart of Zen shines forth. The method is to recite the riddle in one's mind syllable-by-syllable, dwelling upon each syllable with full attention. If the riddle is "The eastern hill keeps running on the water," it would be mentally recited as "The east-ern hill keeps run-ning on the wat-er." Katsuki Sekida explains the effects of such recitation:

When a word or phrase is kept in the mind for a certain length of time, without being mixed with other ingredients, it seems to infiltrate every part of the brain. . . . At our ordinary reading speed no such infiltration normally occurs. But it does sometimes happen when you read the work of a great poet you particularly admire, or read the Bible, dwelling on every word and taking ample time over it. On such an occasion you may be reading word by word, carefully and with deep appreciation, and suddenly the passage will seem charged with infinite meaning, seeming almost to come as a revelation from heaven. Anyone who has ever read the Bible with devoted piety must have had such an experience. We call this sort of reading "language samadhi," and it is this that we must achieve when reciting a Zen koan.[48]

Now we come to the important distinction between Wittgenstein's method of doing philosophy and the method of Zen. Students who enter the Zen environment face a situation that is similar to a huge riddle. The student must find his own way and the intellectual and emotional impasse he experiences just before the moment of enlightenment is triggered by intensive meditation. Meditation is central to Zen. Without it, the Zen environment would not have the desired impact on the student. When Gutei cut off the finger of his student, it was only after the student had come to the brink of enlightenment. All that was needed was a final jolt. But the student had been brought to that high degree of sensitivity through meditation. Nothing similar to meditation exists, however, in Wittgenstein's method.

Because it recognizes the imperfection of words and emphasizes humor, Zen has a built-in system for avoiding dogmatism, and never takes itself too seriously. It is refreshingly iconoclastic. Idols are smashed; wooden statues of the Buddha are burned in winter to keep hands and bodies warm; scriptures are ripped to shreds. Doctrine, tradition, ritual, self, teachers, Gods, and even the Buddha are ruthlessly ridiculed, or laughed into nonexistence.

One of the most sacred moments in Zen is the instant it is said to have been founded. It happened in this way. Gautama Buddha was surrounded by his disciples. Trying to decide which one was to succeed him, he put them to a test. He simply held up a flower. One and only one of his students, Mahākāshyapa, smiled, showing that he had understood the Dharma or teaching; and in this silent manner it has been passed on from generation to generation, like a flower, theoretically independent of words, letters, and scriptures.

III. 35

Because Zen has made a tradition of poking fun at itself, even this most holy scene, the very founding of Zen tradition, is not immune. The silent transmission of the teaching to Mahāk-āshyapa is ridiculed by the master Mumon in these words:

Golden-faced Gautama behaved outrageously. He reduced the sublime to the simple. He sold dog meat for mutton and thought it wonderful to do so. Had the whole congregation smiled, to whom would he have transmitted the right Dharma? Had Mahākāshyaka not smiled, to whom would he have transmitted it? If you say that the right Dharma can be transmitted, the golden-faced old man deceived the world. If it cannot be, how could he give the message even to Mahākāshyapa?[49]

Even greater irreverence is directed against the Buddha. If you should meet the Buddha on the path, Zen advises us, kill him! For if you do not kill him, you will be killed by him. We must *especially* do away with our most sacred idols if we are to be free. The Buddha, like all the other paraphernalia of Buddhism, must be demolished if one is to be a true Buddhist.

What, then, of the Cosmic Axis, somewhat sacred to this book? "On top of a flagpole," goes a famous Zen riddle, "a cow is giving birth to a calf." A student may meditate on this for years before he gives an answer that is accepted by his teacher. When he does satisfy his master with a response, the student is next expected to complete his dissolution of the riddle by choosing from a book containing thousands of short "capping phrases," just one. This book is known almost by heart by all Zen students. If the teacher is satisfied with the phrase selected, the student will then be assigned another riddle. Some of the capping phrases the student might choose from to complete his work on the *koan* are:

Each time you bring it up,
Each time it is new.

If it can't be swallowed, it can't be spit out.

The sacred tortoise drags its tail.

Words fail.

Above the budless branches
The golden phoenix soars.
Around the shadowless tree
The jade elephant circumambulates.

In the spring beyond time
The withered tree flowers.

A difficult choice; and Zen truly begins only when all these choices and word-games end. Enlightenment is not really the goal or culmination of Zen; it is the beginning. Thus when the masters poke fun at Zen, they are only poking fun at the concept of Zen, using concepts. And Zen, whatever "it" is, remains, after all, free of concepts, words, and scriptures.

The image of the Cosmic Tree appears also in the story of the Buddha's awakening. In fact, the tree under which the Great Being gained enlightenment is called the Bo Tree, the Tree of Awakening. Not yet being enlightened, however, he couldn't quite figure out just where under the tree to take his seat. A grass cutter came along, carrying a load of newly cut grass. Seeing the Great Being, and noticing his obvious air of holiness, he gave him several handfuls of grass to sit on. The Future Buddha took the grass and then stood on the southern side of the tree. When he did this the southern half of the world sank into Hell, while the northern half, like the opposite side of a great wheel, touched Heaven. Deciding that this was not the right spot, the Future Buddha walked to the western side of the tree. The western half of the world sank into Hell, and the eastern half, like the opposite side of a great wheel, rose into Heaven. He then proceeded to the northern side, with the same result. Finally he walked around the tree to the eastern side, circumambulating it like an elephant. It is on this eastern side of the tree that all subsequent Buddhas have sat in the Lotus Posture, for that spot is firm and abiding.

Since the Future Buddha thought that this must be the spot, he shook out the grass he held, and it fell upon the ground and formed a beautiful seat, more beautiful than any carver could have fashioned. Then he seated himself, resolving not to move until he had attained supreme wisdom.

In this legend, the world is like a great wheel. At its center is the Bo Tree. To complete the *maṇḍala*, the Future Buddha walks around the tree, facing the *four* directions, and finally situates himself on the eastern side, the very center of the *maṇḍala*.

We have seen that any *maṇḍala* is equivalent to a two-dimensional representation of the Cosmic Tree. It is under this very tree that the Buddha becomes enlightened.

For any student of Zen who meditates with similar resolve on the *koan*, the moment of enlightenment, or *satori*, comes—and usually in an instant. Though it may be triggered by the most trivial event—meditation on a riddle, the raising of a finger, the snap of a twig, or the bottom falling out of a bucket—it is as though the bottom has fallen out of the universe instead; and the student floods into a new universe, just like the old one except that it is beyond words.

Haiku

Zen permeates many aspects of Japanese aesthetics, and especially that most diminutive of Japanese poetic forms known as the *haiku*. The Japanese, it is said, display their genius in small things. A single *haiku*, though comprising only seventeen syllables, may have more poetic impact than entire volumes of less potent verse. Like Patañjali's concise formulas, *mantras*, and *koans*, the inner vastness of the *haiku* is in inverse ratio to its outer form. Like the hut in the following *haiku*,[50] seventeen syllables can contain the whole universe:

In my little bamboo hut this spring,
There is nothing. There is everything.

American *haiku* poets have taken the *haiku* tradition even further in this direction. Cor van den Heuvel has written a *haiku* of just two syllables, which nevertheless fill up an otherwise blank page with their vastness.[51] His work simply reads:

tundra

Creating a world within a *haiku* requires a certain poetic vision. Like the flash of intuition of the Vedic seers or the sudden burst of enlightenment engendered by the *koan,* each *haiku* is like a mini-enlightenment, revealing its depth in a sudden, sometimes blinding, instant of poetic insight. A true master of the art achieves this effect partly through the traditional structure of the form, consisting usually of three lines, though this is not always the case. In the form with three lines, the first introduces a subject. The second line contains a countersubject. Subject and countersubject thus create a polarity, an almost electric disequilibrium. This tension is bridged by the third line, which brings the two together in an unexpected way. An example in English[52] is the following:

There the great bronze Buddha sits;
A swallow
Darts out suddenly from his nostril.

The subject of the first line is the very image of enlightenment, of life beyond the realm of pain and suffering that constitutes this world. But what do we find in the second line! A swallow, the perfect representative of this fleeting world. And so we have a polarity. The great bronze Buddha; a swallow. The state of perfect enlightenment; this world of endless birth, pain, suffering, and death. And yet the ultimate realization in Zen is that this world of everyday life is enlightenment—a realization that comes as swiftly as the dart of a swallow.

The close relationship between Zen and the *haiku* is illustrated in the way the most famous *haiku* of all came to be. There once lived a poet of great renown by the name of Bashō. He lived a very simple life in Japan, wandering from village to village and writing his verse on the basis of his everyday experiences. From time to time he would stay at a Zen monastery, and once when he was studying with a master named Bucchō, the teacher thought that he would test this poet's depth of Zen. He asked Bashō, "How are you doing these days?"

Bashō replied, "After the rain the moss is greener."

Bucchō then fired another question: "Before the moss is greener, what Zen is there?"

Bashō replied: "A frog jumps into water, plop!"

Eventually Bashō added a first line in order to complete the poem, which in its final form sounds something like this:

The old pond, ah!
A frog jumps in—
Ker-plop!

Many words have, of course, been written to interpret this poem, but it is perhaps best left alone, letting its sound be echoed by the silent resonance in these famous lines by Busson:

Just before the stroke of noon
The butterfly snoozes
On the big bronze bell.

The boom of the noon bell, summoning the monks to lunch, is not mentioned, only implied, like the silent thunder in Busson's masterpiece:

Lightning!
The sound of raindrops
Falling among bamboo.

By the end of this poem[53] we are listening to the play of raindrops. It is a false end, however. We have forgotten that at any moment we are going to be overcome by a clap of thunder, which will explode as unexpectedly as the boom of a bell, the ker-plop of a frog, or the bottom falling out of the universe.

Even more silent is the sound of the Buddha, lifting the flower and thereby communicating the essence of Zen to Mahākāshyapa, which is alluded to in these words:[54]

The host was mute.
The guest was dumb.
And silent, too, the white chrysanthemum.

While a *koan* or a *haiku* is not the same as a *sūtra* or a *mantra,* we see in Zen that same tendency of the mind to enter into an increasingly intimate relationship with concise, seemingly useless and nonsensical expressions in order to overcome the bewitchment of language. It is a sort of mental judo in which words throw themselves. Each *koan* and *haiku* is a minute judo master capable of pulling the rug of language out from under our feet. When it clicks, there is a brief flash, as when we get the meaning of a joke. For an instant something vast within us opens, and just as suddenly slams shut, though ripples of meaning echo on like water rings in a pool, and we see into our frog-nature.

As the Zen student enters deeply into Mu or the yogi meditates on Om, the incessant mental dialogue is left speechless and wholeness dawns. Whereas the Vedic seers find reality at the very core of language, in Buddhism language is seen merely as a pointer that must ultimately be transcended. The difference is that the Buddhist view of language is narrower. The Buddhist may have visions, hear inner sounds, and experience immeasurable inner silence as a result of meditation on a *koan,* but he does not consider these inner phenomena to be language. The Vedic seer, on the other hand, considers such experiences to be the inner strata of speech. The difference is only philosophical, and not real.

Riding backwards on an ox,
I enter the Buddha hall.
    —Zen dictum

Zen has its roots in China, where written words are pictures of things. Thus the Buddhist attitude toward symbols is perhaps best demonstrated in "Ten Bulls," a series of paintings that represent ten stages of Zen realization—ten degrees of the relationship of the mind to symbols.[55] The bull (or ox) here represents the Buddha-mind or Buddha-nature, which like the sacred ox of India symbolizes the ultimate—to be sought, conquered, and eventually forgotten. In this process the seeker must learn to discriminate between the *concept* of the Buddha-nature and the Buddha-nature itself. He must eventually forget all about the "ox." Traditionally the ninth of the ten paintings in the series is of a tree.

Ill.   36–1

1. The Search for the Bull
In the pasture of this world, I endlessly push aside the tall grasses
    in search of the bull.
Following unnamed rivers, lost upon the interpenetrating paths
    of distant mountains,
My strength failing and my vitality exhausted, I cannot find the
    bull.
I only hear the locusts chirring through the forest at night.

Comment: The bull never has been lost. What need is there to
search? Only because of separation from my true nature, I fail to
find him. In the confusion of the senses I lose even his tracks. Far
from home, I see many crossroads, but which way is the right one
I know not. Greed and fear, good and bad, entangle me.

Ill. 36–2

2. Discovering the Footprints
Along the riverbank under the trees, I discover footprints!
Even under the fragrant grass I see his prints.
Deep in remote mountains they are found.
These traces no more can be hidden than one's nose, looking
     heavenward.

Comment: Understanding the teaching, I see the footprints of
the bull. Then I learn that, just as many utensils are made from
one metal, so too are myriad entities made of the fabric of self.
Unless I discriminate, how will I perceive the true from the
untrue? Not yet having entered the gate, nevertheless I have
discerned the path.

Ill.   36–3

3. Perceiving the Bull
I hear the song of the nightingale.
The sun is warm, the wind is mild, willows are green along the
    shore,
Here no bull can hide!
What artist can draw that massive head, those majestic horns?

Comment: When one hears the voice, one can sense its source.
As soon as the six senses merge, the gate is entered. Wherever one
enters one sees the head of the bull! This unity is like salt in water,
like color in dyestuff. The slightest thing is not apart from self.

Ill.   36–4

4. Catching the Bull
I seize him with a terrific struggle.
His great will and power are inexhaustible.
He charges to the high plateau far above the cloud-mists,
Or in an impenetrable ravine he stands.

Comment: He dwelt in the forest a long time, but I caught him today! Infatuation for scenery interferes with his direction. Longing for sweeter grass, he wanders away. His midn still is stubborn and unbridled. If I wish him to submit, I must raise my whip.

Ill.   36–5

5. *Taming the Bull*
The whip and rope are necessary,
Else he might stray off down some dusty road.
Being well trained, he becomes naturally gentle.
Then, unfettered, he obeys his master.

Comment: When one thought arises, another thought follows. When the first thought springs from enlightenment, all subsequent thoughts are true. Through delusion, one makes everything untrue. Delusion is not caused by objectivity; it is the result of subjectivity. Hold the nose-ring tight and do not allow even a doubt.

Ill.   36–6

6. *Riding the Bull Home*
Mounting the bull, slowly I return homeward.
The voice of my flute intones through the evening.
Measuring with hand-beats the pulsating harmony, I direct the
    endless rhythm.
Whoever hears this melody will join me.

Comment: This struggle is over; gain and loss are assimilated. I
sing the song of the village woodsman, and play the tunes of the
children. Astride the bull, I observe the clouds above. Onward I
go, no matter who may wish to call me back.

Ill.   36–7

7. The Bull Transcended
Astride the bull, I reach home.
I am serene. The bull too can rest.
The dawn has come. In blissful repose,
Within my thatched dwelling I have abandoned the whip and
    rope.

Comment: All is one law, not two. We only make the bull a
temporary subject. It is as the relation of rabbit and trap, of fish
and net. It is as gold and dross, or the moon emerging from a
cloud. One path of clear light travels on throughout endless time.

Ill.   36–8

8. Both Bull and Self Transcended
Whip, rope, person, and bull—all merge in No-Thing.
This heaven is so vast no message can stain it.
How may a snowflake exist in a raging fire?
Here are the footprints of the patriarchs.

Comment: Mediocrity is gone. Mind is clear of limitation. I seek
no state of enlightenment. Neither do I remain where no enlightenment exists. Since I linger in neither condition, eyes cannot see
me. If hundreds of birds strew my path with flowers, such praise
would be meaningless.

Ill.   36–9A

Ill.   36–9B

9. *Reaching the Source*

Too many steps have been taken returning to the root and the
source.
Better to have been blind and deaf from the beginning!
Dwelling in one's true abode, unconcerned with that without—
The river flows tranquilly on and the flowers are red.

Comment: From the beginning, truth is clear. Poised in silence,
I observe the forms of integration and disintegration. One who
is not attached to "form" need not be "reformed." The water
is emerald, the mountain *is* indigo, and I see that which *is*
creating and that which *is* destroying.

Ill.   36–10

10. In the World
Barefooted and naked of breast, I mingle with the people of the
   world.
My clothes are ragged and dust-laden, and I am ever blissful.
I use no magic to extend my life;
Now, before me, the dead trees become alive.

Comment: Inside my gate, a thousand sages do not know me. The
beauty of my garden is invisible. Why should one search for the
footprints of the patriarchs? I go to the market place with my
wine bottle and return home with my staff. I visit the wineshop
and the market, and everyone I look upon becomes enlightened.

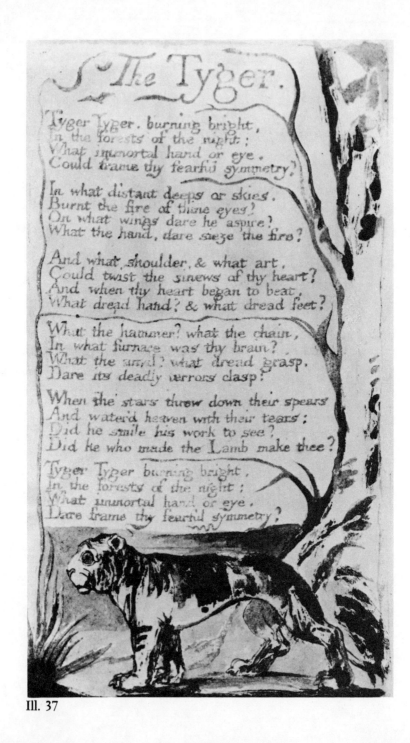

The Tyger.

Tyger Tyger. burning bright,
In the forests of the night;
What immortal hand or eye.
Could frame thy fearful symmetry?

In what distant deeps or skies.
Burnt the fire of thine eyes?
On what wings dare he aspire?
What the hand, dare sieze the fire?

And what shoulder, & what art,
Could twist the sinews of thy heart?
And when thy heart began to beat,
What dread hand? & what dread feet?

What the hammer? what the chain,
In what furnace was thy brain?
What the anvil? what dread grasp.
Dare its deadly terrors clasp?

When the stars threw down their spears
And water'd heaven with their tears:
Did he smile his work to see?
Did he who made the Lamb make thee?

Tyger Tyger burning bright,
In the forests of the night;
What immortal hand or eye.
Dare frame thy fearful symmetry?

Ill. 37

Tyger

23 May, 1810, found the Word Golden.

— WILLIAM BLAKE, manuscript notebook

I magine for a moment a realm flatter than a flounder, a pancake, or even this page—the domain of Flatland.[56] Imagine that you are a Circle in Flatland, a creature living in a two-dimensional universe, who suddenly confronts something you have never seen before—a full-bodied young Sphere. Sure, you've been around. But never before have you seen the sumptuous curvature of this Sphere, which you can never really experience until you are lifted from Flatland up into the realm of three dimensions, until suddenly you grow into a full-fledged Sphere yourself. At this point, however, you become somewhat Cinderella-like. Though you may attend a magnificent ball, you realize that eventually you must return to the humble estate of your former two-dimensional plane. How will you ever be able to tell anyone back home about it? Your story will be as incomprehensible as it is inexpressible. If you speak to the Flatlanders of a realm that is UP, they will only think of north. "Upward, not northward!" you will repeat, vainly gesturing with your hand, frustrated that it only succeeds in pointing northward. It is hopeless; Flatlanders have no way of understanding UP. You feel frustrated. If you are lucky they will admire you as someone talking above their heads, but it is more likely that they will only lift their eyebrows, thinking you are one of those who march to the beat of a different drummer.

The Flatlanders are playing a different language-game than you. You are playing in three dimensions, and they are playing in only two. When such a change in language-games occurs, the *meaning* of the vocabulary changes. UP becomes something different for you than for them. Wittgenstein said that there are innumerable language-games, like various ways of drumming or painting, singing or dancing. And it is difficult to dance a Strauss waltz with someone who insists on dancing the two-step.

Some language-games are, at times, more useful or appropriate than others. Praying, writing a report, lying, and joking all have their time and place. Yet we can pray about joking, joke about praying, lie about writing a report about joking about praying, and so forth. Suppose we were measuring space and time. Mathematics would *perhaps* be a more useful or appropriate language to employ than conversational speech. The Greek philosopher Zeno of Elea, a disciple of Parmenides, was a composer of riddles. One of these, concerning Achilles and a tortoise, illustrates the point.

Achilles and the tortoise are going to run a race. This takes place, we must remember, in ancient Greece, an athletic civilization that was, however, unacquainted with the concept of aerobic exercise, and runners didn't jog but actually raced—albeit against reptiles. At any rate, Achilles is a swift runner; he can run ten times faster than the tortoise. And he is a good sportsman, good enough to give the tortoise a hundred-yard lead. Yet, according to Zeno, Achilles will never catch up with the tortoise.

The race starts. Achilles runs one hundred yards, but the tortoise has already covered one tenth of that distance and is therefore ten yards ahead. Achilles then runs these ten yards. But now the tortoise has run one more yard. Achilles runs this yard.

But by now the tortoise has run one tenth of a yard farther. By the time Achilles covers this distance, the tortoise has covered another hundredth of a yard. And so the story continues, *ad infinitum*. Achilles will never quite catch up with the tortoise, though he will get nearer and nearer. Or so it would seem in ordinary language.

Suppose, though, we employ mathematical language to express the distance covered by the tortoise. We can write it in fractions, as follows:

10 + 1 + 1/10 + 1/100 + 1/1,000 + 1/10,000 + 1/100,000 . . .

or in decimals:

10 + 1 + 0.1 + 0.01 + 0.001 + 0.0001 . . .

which adds up to:

11.11111111 . . .

or, more elegantly, 11.i yards.

The symbol 0.i means 1/9. Thus the tortoise will travel precisely 11 1/9 yards before he is passed by Achilles. Because mathematical language is so successful in measuring such things, it is used universally. It solves riddles and other problems. We send men to the moon and they land right on target. Mathematics, though, like every other type of language, exerts a certain tyranny over us. In the very act of measuring, we find ourselves measured.

Consider the painting entitled "Newton" by the poet and engraver William Blake. The power and beauty of Newton's frame are distorted by the act of measuring; his torso and limbs become a parody of the very shape he gauges. His limbs assume a contracted, angular form. His sinuous strength is shriveled to the austere dimensions of the plane he surveys. He is like a Sphere, a three-dimensional being, reduced to the two dimensions of Flatland. He is, in the final analysis, like the stone on which he sits. He is petrified humanity, and the task of the poet is to get this stone to speak divine words.

Blake was something of a four-dimensional man—a visionary who as a youth beheld the face of God pressing against the

Ill. 38

window of his house. At the age of eight or ten, as he rambled
through the open meadows and hedgerows near his home, he saw
a tree filled with angels. On another dewy summer's morn he saw
haymowers at work, with angelic beings floating among them. It
is little wonder that he rebelled so vehemently against the merely
three-dimensional, mechanical world view that Newton's physics
had popularized, and that reigned in physics until the appearence
of Einstein in the twentieth century. Blake's vision of the universe
and criticism of Newton's classical physics has much in common
with Einstein's insights and revision of the Newtonian model of
the universe. In fact, Blake's critique is essentially anticipatory of
the vision of relativity physics, especially in regard to the nature
of the space-time continuum.

Newton's way of looking at things did not begin with Newton. The Greek philosopher Democritus was born in Abdera, in
Thrace, about 460 B.C. He lived to an advanced age, writing

prolifically on the theories of his teacher Leucippus—little aware that these very theories would contribute to the tyranny of measurement over man that Blake's "Newton" portrays. Democritus believed that the Infinite manifests atoms, which split off from it, giving rise to a vortex motion. Within this vortex, the atoms swarm about like bees, mixing with one another and finally giving rise to the world. The atoms, which are the minutest, indivisible units of matter, are inert and passive—responsive only to spiritual forces that are completely separate from them.

Such a view, in which spirit is irreconcilably cut off from matter, accomplished in one blow the complete demythologization of nature. No longer can Zeus *be* the oak tree and the thunder, Apollo the laurel, Neptune the ruler of the sea. No longer can the voices of water nymphs be heard in brooks, springs, and fountains. "We have drained the light from the boughs in the sacred grove," says Annie Dillard, "and snuffed it in the high places and along the banks of sacred streams." This disenchantment of the world was amplified in the Western world with the idea of a Judeo-Christian God who utterly transcends creation—so that by the seventeenth century René Descartes was easily able to popularize the notion of a mind-matter dualism, a cleavage of ourselves from ourselves, which in turn made Newton's views possible. For Newton's model of the universe was one consisting of inert matter completely separate from humanity, and divinity. The universe, for Newton, was a vast machine ruled from above by a God, but separate from Him. To discover the laws of this universe was to discover the eternal, invariable laws of God.

In 1666, the story goes, Isaac Newton was snoozing under an apple (rather than a Bo) tree, and had a rather rude awakening when, suddenly, an apple fell on his head. Thus he began to think about gravity, and formulated equations that express its force between two bodies, including not only the Earth and an apple but the Earth and the Moon, and other celestial bodies. His work formed the basis of classical physics, the mechanistic world view that was not seriously challenged in the realm of science until the beginning of this century, when Einstein's insights ushered in a more holistic, organic, and subtle way of talking about events in nature.

Just like Democritus, Newton envisioned atomistic, indestructible material particles moving about in a three-dimensional space that remains essentially unchanged, flowing evenly and as rigidly as clock time flows from the past through the present to the future. Everything that happens in such a universe is due to the motion of immutable particles of matter attracted to one another by the force of gravity.

Newtonian measurement depends upon the integrity of mass that is not distorted as it moves through space, and space that is absolute. This is space in which objects do not change depending upon the direction in which they move. Furthermore, Newton's measurement depends upon invariable units of length with which to measure, which in turn depend upon an observer whose perception remains constant as such measurements are taken. In other words, measurement in classical physics depends upon notions of space and time much as they are experienced in everyday life, and such a system of measurement proves to be highly successful. It can account for planetary and thermal motion. Immutable space and time are the *containers* of equally fixed physical particles. Space and time form a stage on which these particles move about according to the predictable force of gravity guided by the hand of God.

Imagine, however, that as we carry a table into the kitchen from the dining room, the table expands. Now imagine that we also expand as we walk into the kitchen, and that everything else expands right along with us. If we take along a ruler to measure things, the ruler has expanded as much as the table, and the table thus measures precisely the same! In such an instance, we would have no way of knowing that we had expanded or that anything else had. If, however, we could somehow step outside this whole picture as we do when we say, "Imagine . . ." then we could see what is really happening—at least from *our* point of view. We could see that the unit of measurement, the ruler, which seems to stay so fixed, and even the table it measures are very fluid indeed.

In 1905 Albert Einstein pulled the rug out from under the Newtonian table as he began to see time, space, matter, and energy in much the same way as the Circle leaving Flatland expanded into a new world. Einstein replaced Newton's notion of absolute time, a steady stream of time flowing immutably from past to future. Einstein said that like the sense of taste or sight, the sense of time is a class of perception. And that is not all. Time and space are no longer two separate, absolute entities, but are joined together in a four-dimensional space-time continuum. In Einstein's new language of relativity theory, we cannot speak of space without including time, and vice versa. Space-time language is the language a particular observer uses to describe what is seen from a certain perspective. One observer may see two events happening simultaneously, while another observer, moving with a different velocity relative to the events, will see them happening at different times.

Imagine now, if you will, that we are sitting at a railroad station. A train passes. The man we see through the window of the dining car is just cutting into his steaming platter of French toast. From our perspective the French toast is speeding past at sixty miles per hour. For the man in the dining car it is sitting still.

The light of the sun reaches us in eight minutes. The nearest star is four light-years away. When we gather the light of the galaxies into our massive telescopes, we look out on the past, seeing the galaxies as they actually were millions of years ago. Depending as does perception upon the observer, a universal picture of the universe as it exists at this instant is impossible, according to relativity physics.

Like space and time, matter and energy are no longer seen as isolated entities. In Einstein's equation $E = mc^2$, mass is nothing but a knot of energy. This makes it possible to understand a nuclear war as a slipknot, with two or more nations playing tug-of-war.

Furthermore, space-time and matter-energy are not separate

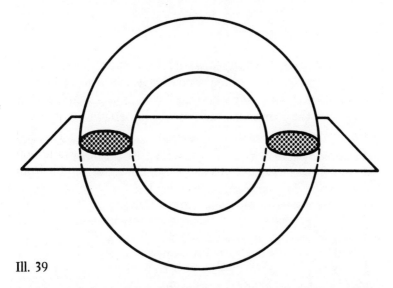

Ill. 39

but unified. The very nature of space-time depends on the distri-
bution of matter. In the presence of a massive body such as a
planet or a star, the surrounding space-time becomes curved, and
is thus variable in various parts of the universe.

How can space and time, or matter and energy, be one thing
instead of two? Consider a doughnut's encounter with Flatland.
An observer in two-dimensional Flatland sees only two circles,
whereas an observer in three dimensions sees only one doughnut.

It was just such a unified but poetic vision that prompted
Blake's critique of Newton. Newton's exact measurement and
rigid notions of time, space, matter, and energy Blake saw as great
evils. And the poet anticipated Einstein's revision of classical
physics, though in the language of poetry rather than that of
physics. Indeed, Blake presented a critique of Newton's language.

For Blake all time is present in each moment. He proclaims,
"I see the Past, Present & Future existing all at once/Before
me."[57] Or he sees with divine vision the seven eyes of God,
whether sitting down within

The plowed furrow, list'ning to the weeping clods till we
Contract or Expand Space at will, or if we raise ourselves
Upon the chariots of the morning, Contracting or Expanding Time,
Every one knows we are One Family, One Man blessed for ever.[58]

In these passages Newton's absolute time and absolute space dissolve, shrinking or swelling according to the will of eternal Man. For Blake, clock time is corrupt, fallen time descended from eternity and the luminous timelessness of poetic vision.

> . . . Moments & Minutes & Hours
> And Days & Months & Years & Ages & Periods, wondrous buildings;
> And every Moment has a Couch of gold for soft repose,
> (A Moment equals a pulsation of the artery),
> And between every two Moments stands a Daughter of Beulah
> To feed the Sleepers on their Couches with maternal care.
> And every Minute has an azure Tent with silken Veils:
> And every Hour has a bright golden Gate carved with skill:
> And every Day & Night has Walls of brass & Gates of adamant,
> Shining like precious Stones & ornamented with appropriate signs:
> And every Month a silver paved Terrace builded high:
> And every Year invulnerable Barriers with high Towers:
> And every Age is Moated deep with Bridges of silver & gold:
> And every Seven Ages is Incircled with a Flaming Fire.
> Now Seven Ages is amounting to Two Hundred Years.
> Each has its Guard, each Moment, Minute, Hour, Day, Month &
>   Year.[59]

Here eternity solidifies into mechanical, inhuman, armored and discrete units. Yet there are as many gates and bridges as there are barriers and moats, and they open to a humane eternity dancing behind the veil of time. Viewed by the fallen, this clock is opaque, but viewed with the faculty of poetic vision, it opens to timelessness and is equally permeable to time and eternity. Blake says of fallen man that

Times on times he divided & measur'd
Space by space in his ninefold darkness,
Unseen, unknown.[60]

Space is measured simultaneously with time. In the following lines, Newton's rigid matter is seen by Blake as nothing but the solidified *energy* of the imagination, just as Einstein saw all matter as energy. The passage is a conversation with "Seven Angels." One of them informs us that

. . . those combin'd by Satan's Tyranny, first in the blood of War
And Sacrifice & next in Chains of imprisonment, are Shapeless Rocks
Retaining only Satan's Mathematic Holiness, Length, Bredth &
    Highth,
Calling the Human Imagination, which is the Divine Vision & Fruition
In which Man liveth eternally, madness & blasphemy against
Its own Qualities, which are Servants of Humanity, not Gods or Lords.
Distinguish therefore States from Individuals in those States.
States Change, but Individual Identities never change nor cease.[61]

Space maintains its identity only by virtue of a fixed set of
mathematical coordinates by which to measure it. But one of the
axioms of Einstein's theory of relativity is that there are an infinite
number of coordinates—or, as Blake prefers, "States"—by which
to measure. We live, then, not within the boundaries of a physical
world, but within the boundaries of our perception of it, especially
as mediated by the coordinates of language.

At the end of the poem *Jerusalem,* as we will see below, "the
Four Living Creatures, Chariots of Humanity Divine Incomprehensible," while creating and dissolving space and time at will,
release awesome brightness and energy "in Visionary forms dramatic which bright/Redounded from their Tongues in thunderous majesty, in Visions/In new Expanses." Einstein's $E = mc^2$
is found here in poetic idiom, energy and form transformed at the
speed of light, a speed at which distinctions between time and
space break down.

Blake's vision differed from Einstein's, however, in at least
one important way. Einstein saw his theories as supplementary to
Newton's. It was not that Newton was wrong and that he was
right—both were right within their own contexts. For Blake,
however, Newton was totally wrong—and despite Blake's similari-
ties to the New Physics, he would certainly recoil from such terms
as "quantum mechanics" and even "physics." He was concerned
with quality, not quantity, and therefore expressed an either-or
attitude concerning the two. He did not realize the the human
mind has the capacity for acute analysis and reasoning one moment and deep intuition the next.

Blake's Einsteinian world is a world of visionary *speech,* of the speech that the Vedic bards also spoke of as thunderous and bright. Blake *sees* this speech. And when this visionary speech is born, the worlds come into existence. It is like the biblical vision of John:

In the beginning was the Word,
And the Word was with God,
And the Word was God.

As the Word is measured, so is the world, and humanity. Blake's criticism of Newton is essentially a criticism of quantitive language, logic, reason, and "Mathematic Holiness." Whereas the eighteenth-century cult of reason saw objective sense experience and reason as the valid means to knowledge, Blake protested that the intuition or imagination was as sure a guide. Absolute space and time and the entire Newtonian universe, which Blake saw as distorting the minds and bodies of humanity, were willed into existence and accepted as common currency by nothing more nor less than language. The Fall of humanity from eternal delight into error and sin is nothing but the fragmentation of the eternal Word into words.

Like the poetry of the Vedic seers of India, Blake's poetry is largely descriptive of language. In fact, one expert on Blake goes so far as to say that "everything Blake says about Man, the Universe, society, imagination and the senses—in fact, everything that he says about anything—is translatable into a comment upon language, words, the poet's task, poetry."[62] And we find within Blake's poetry the four levels of language, from eternal silence to articulate syllables, spoken of by the Vedic seers.

THE LANGUAGE OF ETERNITY

Normally when we speak of *eternal silence,* we distinguish it from *infinite space.* Like Newton we tend to separate time and space into discrete categories. In Blake's poetry, however, Eternity is spoken of as a *place,* and has a spatial, though infinite, dimension. Eternity is then something of a nontemporal land-scape. For Blake, as for Einstein, space-time is a continuum. Eternity is not the endless duration of time. It is the absence of time.

Blake does not tell us much about this level of language. He does write, however, that

When in Eternity Man converses with Man, they enter
Into each other's Bosom (which are Universes of delight)
In mutual interchange.[63]

This suggests the friendship among the Vedic seers due to their ability to see the best, purest, primordial core of the Word. We must realize that Blake was a visionary, not a saint. He was concerned with that level of language where formlessness emerges into form, the language of vision.

THE LANGUAGE OF THE SOUND-LIGHT CONTINUUM

Language and the world emerge from a luminous, thunder-ous cauldron in which words and worlds are forged. In this fiery light fallen language is redeemed. The Vedic seers spoke of the four directions and all of space-time as springing forth from the Word. Blake writes of the reverse of this process, the Apocalypse, when the world withdraws into a fourfold *maṇḍala* of reintegration.

The Four Living Creatures, Chariots of Humanity Divine Incompre-
    hensible,
In beautiful Paradises expand. These are the Four Rivers of Paradise
And the Four Faces of Humanity, fronting the Four Cardinal Points
Of Heaven, going forward, forward irresistible from Eternity to Eter-
    nity.
And they conversed together in Visionary forms dramatic which bright
Redounded from their Tongues in thunderous majesty, in Visions
In new Expanses, creating exemplars of Memory and of Intellect,
Creating Space, Creating Time, according to the wonders Divine
Of Human Imagination throughout all the Three Regions immense

Of Childhood, Manhood & Old Age; & the all tremendous unfathoma-
   ble Non Ens
Of Death was seen in regenerations terrific or complacent, varying
According to the subject of discourse; & every Word & Every Character
Was Human according to the Expansion or Contraction, the Translu-
   cence or
Opakeness of Nervous fibres: such was the variation of Time & Space
Which vary according as the Organs of Perception vary; & they walked
To & fro in Eternity as One Man, reflecting each in each & clearly seen
And seeing, according to fitness & order. And I heard Jehovah speak
Terrific from his Holy Place, & saw the Words of the Mutual Covenant
   Divine
On Chariots of gold & jewels, with Living Creatures, starry & flaming
With every Colour, Lion, Tyger, Horse, Elephant, Eagle, Dove, Fly,
   Worm.[64]

   This is clearly the language of vision, of the sound-light
continuum, where the four primal creative powers *converse* in
visionary forms, which are *bright* and *thundering*. Thunder,
sound, name and vision, light, form are united in lightning-speech
that *creates* what it names rather than merely describing, pointing, or referring. Yet every word and every character was human.
Time-space varies according to the purity of the human nervous
system and its organs of perception.
   The fourfold shape of the vision forms a sacred enclosure, a
maṇḍala in which the psyche may find a center. In the poem
Jerusalem, Blake symbolizes this reintegration by the reunion of
Man (whom he calls Albion) with his inner, loving, caring, and
intuitive nature (which he calls Jerusalem). Albion and Jerusalem
must unite. The intuitive qualities, as they become established in
the personality, bring with them an extraordinary sense of wholeness. This is often revealed in dreams and visions that contain
certain invariable elements of design. As we have noted above, the
maṇḍala appears as a circle, either divided in four parts or enclosed within a square. Often at its center is the Cosmic Tree.
Blake has painted with his words thus far a square—the Four
Zoas.

In this same poem, ending in quadernity, we find the holy
of holies, the center of the *maṇḍala*. The Cosmic Axis appears
not as a tree but as the maiden Jerusalem.

I see thy Form, O lovely mild Jerusalem, Wing'd with Six Wings
In the opacous Bosom of the Sleeper, lovely Three-fold
In Head & Heart & Reins, three Universes of love & beauty.
Thy forehead bright, Holiness to the Lord, with Gates of pearl
Reflects Eternity; beneath, thy azure wings of feathery down
Ribb'd delicate & cloth'd with feather'd gold & azure & purple,
From thy white shoulders shadowing purity in holiness!
Thence, feather'd with soft crimson of the ruby, bright as fire,
Spreading into the azure, Wings which like a canopy
Bends over thy immortal Head in which Eternity dwells."[65]

Lovely Jerusalem, the intuitive power of humanity, stands like a
celestial pillar. Above her is the azure canopy of her feathers. And
at the center of this shines her immortal head in which Eternity
dwells. The symbolism of the crown *chakra*, with which we are
by now so familiar, is evident. And this is followed, a few lines
later, by a vision of the Tree of Life and the River of Life and
a divine pillar. In this fourth chapter of the poem Blake thus
completes the *maṇḍala*.

This is, however, the language of the sound-light continuum,
and this vision has its sonorous aspect. In the same section that
paints for us the Tree of Life and the divine pillar, we are told
that Jerusalem is adorned with

Bells of silver round [her] knees living articulate
Comforting sounds of love & harmony.[66]

It seems that we have seen this picture painted earlier in this
volume. Someone deft with a brush and India ink has already
painted a vision that is all feathered wings, with sounding bells
crowning the central pillar of adoration.

Ironically, it was the same vision, the Cosmic Tree, that
haunted Newton. At the opening of his discussion of gravity
Newton advances, as his first hypothesis, the view that the center

of the system of the world is immovable, and he envisions the heavens turning about this axis.

The difference is that Blake's central figure flourishes in its proper clime, the domain of visionary language, while Newton quantifies this form and ascribes it to the physical rather than the intuitive cosmos.

The Atoms of Democritus
And Newton's Particles of light
Are sands upon the Red sea shore
Where Israel's tents do shine so bright.[67]

While Newton's atomistic particles of light are set in motion by outside forces, Blake's inner light is creative in and of itself, giving form to things and setting them in motion. Newton's atomistic particles of light are mere sands that gleam only when illumined by an exterior light—compared to the tents of Israel, the inner light that shines from within itself.

By the power of language the bards of yore created all forms simply by naming them.

The ancient Poets animated all sensible objects with Gods or Geniuses, calling them by the names and adorning them with the properties of woods, rivers, mountains, lakes, cities, nations, and whatever their enlarged & numerous senses could perceive.

ᷩ   And particularly they studied the genius of each city & country, placing it under its mental deity;

Till a system was formed, which some took advantage of, & enslav'd the vulgar by attempting to realize or abstract the mental deities from their objects: thus began Priesthood;

Choosing forms of worship from poetic tales.

And at length they pronounc'd that the Gods had order'd such things.

Thus men forgot that All deities reside in the human breast.[68]

The ancient poets speak in the name-form continuum. Thus in the act of speaking or calling, sensible objects are created, are named, and are divine. The poetic universe of unity of name and form holds the subject, the name, the deity, and the object to-

gether—they are all one unified experience. But when the illuminative Word falls, it fragments—subject, object, and deity are
divided from one another. The object is now dead Newtonian
matter. The name is only a word. The subject, if not endowed
with poetic vision, needs the priest to join all together again. And
thus all the Gods are seen in churches and temples rather than
in the human breast, where the human heart pulses. And

Every Time less than a pulsation of the artery
Is equal in its period & value to Six Thousand Years,
For in this Period the Poet's Work is Done: and all the Great
Events of Time start forth & are conceiv'd in such a Period,
Within a Moment, a Pulsation of the Artery.[69]

The art of the poet is accomplished in the pulse of an artery, in
a flash of poetic vision.

On this level of language, the level of the sound-light continuum, Blake finds the fulfillment of experience. For here experience is totally innocent. Experience does not overshadow innocence. The flow of images does not overshadow Eternity. It is like
the yogic technique of *samyama*, in which the object of attention
is seen in the light of the Eternal. On this level, each experience
is full in its individuality and in its universality. Each song of
experience is a song of innocence.

THE LANGUAGE OF THOUGHTS

Normally we appreciate the luminous forms of Eternity only
after they have become the pale, shadowy forms of thoughts, and
have become institutionalized in forms of worship. This is the
domain of the priest rather than the poet. The Word, as it falls
and fragments becomes thought,

Dark, revolving in silent activity:
Unseen in tormenting passions:
An activity unknown and horrible,
A self-contemplating shadow,
In enormous labours occupied.[70]

THE LANGUAGE OF WORDS

Finally, we have the spoken English tongue, which Blake termed the "rough basement," the medium through which poet and Word must awaken the reader. Though Blake writes in English, he departs from the discursive monotony of prose, especially Newton's mathematical language. Blake abandons reason and logic, presenting us with a series of images in jumbled syntax.

Reason and the rational power of logical argument was, for Blake, the antithesis of art and imagination; it was the very embodiment of the fallen, fragmented form of the Word. His poetry is no less than a war against the language of philosophy and science, which has a legacy dating back to the Greeks.

The method of the Greek philosopher Zeno depended entirely on logic. If Zeno's opponent took the position that Achilles would pass the tortoise in a matter of yards, Zeno simply presented the logical steps of his argument and won the debate every time. Eventually his opponent had to abandon his position, even though in a real race, Achilles would have won every time. Logic in this case wins only a debate. It proves Zeno right, though he is obviously in error.

Zeno's influence was great, however. The early dialogues of Plato have the same form. Socrates allows his friends to take a position on some subject; then he questions them quite logically, eventually leading them to abandon their original position because it is inconsistent with the logical outcome of the dialogue.

Thrasymachus, for example, is asked by Socrates in *The Republic* what the nature of justice is. He answers that justice is always to the advantage of the stronger. Socrates leads his opponent to refute his own statement by a logical cross-examination in which Thrasymachus admits that science does not seek its own advantage, and that all forms of rule are sciences. Therefore the ruler, who is stronger, cannot seek his own advantage.

Plato's student Aristotle further systematized logic and thereby deeply influenced the entire Western tradition of thought. Not for two thousand years would logic be seen as a technique of debate, a game often used to prove rather than discover something.

Such language is the fall of the eternal, nonsequential syntax of the Word, the fall of the visionary forms into mere terms—words nested neatly in their proper time- and space-bound grammatical sequence, in a line on a page. Blake redeems the Word by breaking up the normal patterns of English. He voices a new language in order to annihilate the dehumanized world created by Newton's language. Blake proclaims:

I rest not from my great task!
To open the Eternal Worlds, to open the immortal Eyes
Of Man inwards into the Worlds of Thought, into Eternity
Ever expanding in the Bosom of God, the Human Imagination.[71]

To open "the Eternal Worlds," to break the bewitchment of language and transmute space and time into Eternity, Blake shifts the tenses of his verbs and creates a convoluted syntax and chaotic ordering of events that shake away our normal, linear, language-bound picture of the world. He employs paradox and metaphor to numb the three-dimensional mind, and he presents beautiful verbal icons of the domain of visionary speech.

The awareness of the reader is as important as that of the poet. For according to Blake, "every Word & Every Character/ [Is] Human according to the Expansion or Contraction, the Translucence or/Opakeness" of our "Nervous fibres." His poetry unfolds itself according to the purity of the nervous system of the reader.

If the Spectator could Enter into these Images in his Imagination, approaching them on the Fiery Chariot of his Contemplative Thought, if he could Enter into Noah's Rainbow or into his bosom, or could make a Friend & Companion of one of these Images of wonder, which always intreats him to leave mortal things (as he must know), then would he arise from his Grave, then would he meet the Lord in the Air & then he would be happy.[72]

Then we would see that the Flood and the Apocalypse and Christ and the Buddha and the Cosmic Tree are present to us in words, as a verbal presence. When we play religion we find our minds and hearts emptied, for a moment, of secular images as we paint a world of angels, Gods, and Saviors. We replace one set of pictures with another set that is highly emotionally charged and reinforced by our society and dogma. We must see deeply into these words and images, however, if they are not to become our masters. It is our *relationship* to the symbol, the Word, that is important. As the Vedic seers advise, the Goddess of the Word reveals herself to those who love her. Such lovers become seers of the Word. Among those who see only words, there is strife and death. Words become weapons.

Yet, as the Muṇḍaka Upanishad states:

The syllable Om is the bow; the soul is the arrow;
God is the target.
By meditating on Om undistractedly, one is to hit the target.
One is to hit the target, like an arrow.[73]

On November 22, 1802, Blake penned similar lines:

With the bows of my Mind & the Arrows of Thought—
My bowstring fierce with Ardour breathes,
My arrows glow in their golden sheaves.[74]

So often in Blake, inner illumination shines with the same golden radiance that is represented by the central point of Indian *maṇḍalas,* and that is called Hiranyagarbha—"the Golden Egg." In strictly geometric *maṇḍalas* such as *yantras,* this Golden Egg is represented by the dot in the center, the bull's-eye. Less often the dot is represented by drawing a golden ellipse or egg form against an empty background.

From this Golden Embryo shining in the void, the entire creation springs forth. Because this womb supports all beings it is called *dhāraṇi* (and here we have another relative of the ancient Proto-Indo-European oak term), "that which supports." Its pla-

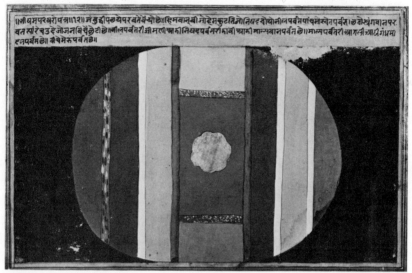

Ill. 40

centa is said to be Mount Meru, and in its center, steadfast as an
oak, stands a majestic tree. This Golden Egg is the most intimate
manifestation of formless, colorless, invisible Eternity, the most
subtle level of the sound-light continuum.

Blake's method is more revolutionary, critical, and destructive than it is creative. The redemption of fallen humanity, the
revelation of innocence, and the dawning of Eternity require, as
in Christianity, nothing short of an Apocalypse—which takes
place within the fiery forge of the visionary forms, in the cauldron
of the inner Word, golden and growling. This growling gold
destroys to create light and enfold the poet in its rays.

My eyes more & more
Like a Sea without shore
Continue Expanding,
The Heavens commanding,
Till the Jewels of Light,
Heavenly Men beaming bright,
Appear'd as One man

Who Complacent began
My limbs to infold
In his beams of bright gold;
Like dross purg'd away
All my mire & my clay.
Soft consum'd in delight
In His bosom Sun bright
I remain'd. Soft he smil'd,
And I heard his voice Mild
Saying: This is My Fold,
O thou Ram horn'd with gold,
Who awakest from Sleep
On the Sides of the Deep.
On the Mountains around
The roarings resound
Of the lion & wolf,
The loud Sea & deep gulf.
These are guards of My Fold,
O thou Ram horn'd with gold![75]

The poet is not only bathed in light, he is consumed. And what strange beast is at once golden, illuminating, and consuming?

Tyger! Tyger! burning bright
In the forests of the night,
What immortal hand or eye
Could frame thy fearful symmetry?[76]

The wrath of Blake's poetic vision is a Tiger. It is the consuming wrath of the divine, fiery forge of the Apocalypse in which all words are purified by light and all worlds are purified by flame. In India the Goddess Durgā, the Terrible Goddess who each autumn drinks the blood of eight hundred goats slaughtered in her honor, is said to be hard to approach. She is difficult to approach because she is, in one of her fiercest forms, the tumeric-yellow, flaming Goddess of Fire. And she is the tiger, whose orange-yellow pelt flames as she stalks her prey. To paint her one paints a tiger *maṇḍala*, in much the same way as Blake paints a tiger with words. He also painted a picture of a tiger, to illustrate his famous poem (see page 154), which looks extremely lamblike. The ferocity of Blake's style opens ultimately to the innocence of the lamb. As Blake entered into words, into the flame of the Word, we now enter the flame of the *maṇḍala*. The still point at the center is light, yellow as lotus pollen, the embryo of the worlds; and we enter it to emerge in another world.

Ill. 41

Kiva

The flames ascend, yellow as corn pollen, sucked fiercely upward through the smoke hole. The smoke rises above the trees, is caught in an upper current of air, and is whirled away. In the chill moonless night the galaxies glimmer above a cloudless sky. Around the fire the room is fragrant with the pungence of burning spruce boughs. Faces bathe in the warmth of the glowing light, and someone named Spider Woman is singing this song:

The dark purple light rises in the north,
A yellow light rises in the east.
Then we of the flowers of the earth come forth
To receive a long life of joy.
We call ourselves the Butterfly Maidens.

Both male and female make their prayers to the east,
Make the respectful sign to the Sun our Creator.
The sounds of bells ring through the air,

Making a joyful sound throughout the land,
Their joyful echo resounding everywhere.

Humbly I ask my Father,
The perfect one, Taiowa, our Father,
The perfect one creating the beautiful life
Shown to us by the yellow light,
To give us perfect light at the time of the red light.

The perfect one laid out the perfect plan
And gave to us a long span of life,
Creating song to implant joy in life.
On this path of happiness, we the Butterfly Maidens
Carry out his wishes by greeting our Father Sun.

The song resounds back from our Creator with joy,
And we of the earth repeat it to our Creator.
At the appearing of the yellow light,
Repeats and repeats again the joyful echo,
Sounds and resounds for times to come.[77]

This is the song Spider Woman sang to the First People of the First World. These First People were the very distant ancestors of the Hopi Indians of the American Southwest. The name "Hopi" itself means "good in every way"—moral, poised, nonaggressive, modest, and peaceful. And that is how this quiet agricultural society lived, surrounded by nomadic enemy tribes. Their view of the universe, inherent in the structure of their language, has much in common with how modern physics views things.

Whereas physicists speaking Indo-European languages have had to invent a new language to talk about such things as the space-time continuum, speakers of Hopi cannot speak or even think of space without speaking of time. In fact, the Hopi language, and its tendency to speak of space-time, is intimately linked with their concept of the Cosmic Axis.

The English language is based on names and objects. We say, "The light flashed." In this sentence, "light" is a noun and "flashed" is, of course, a verb in the past tense. Thus we talk about objects, using nouns, and what happens to them, using verbs. And we use past, present, or future tenses. The Hopi language, however, like modern physics and Buddhist philosophy, treats phenomena as *events* or *happenings* rather than as *objects*. In Hopi there is therefore a fondness for verbs. Instead of saying, "The light flashed," they simply describe it as an event by saying, *"Reh-pi!"*—"Flash!"

How do events—such as the dawning of day, the gradual formation of thunderclouds, the falling of rain, and the growing of plants—happen? The Hopi say that events are prepared and emerge from deep within the heart of all things, which is the heart of nature, of human beings, of plants and animals. This heart is not the physical organ but a subjective, inner realm. It is conceived of as a vertical, vibratory inner axis. Before events happen in the objective world of the senses, they dwell in this heart, along with thoughts and desires. Therefore thoughts and desires play a very big role in the Hopi universe. They are the most powerful, earliest, and most subtle way of preparing events.

Suppose, for instance, that the members of a Hopi tribe want rain for their corn crop. They do not just think in a haphazard fashion, "Gee, I sure wish it would rain." In order for the rain to come, it must be prepared. Everyone gets involved.

The preparing may involve dancing and singing or other community events such as ceremonial smoking. Such acts serve to focus thought and desire so that they can act as very real forces affecting the crops, the clouds, and the formation of rain. For a cloud is not a thing external to the human mind. It is an event that is always in a state of getting later or growing, of transformation. The process of the cloud, clouding, emerges at every moment in a new way. Before clouding emerges on the objective level of the senses it dwells in the heart of all things with desires and thoughts. Thus intense, concentrated thought can influence clouding.

The more intense the thought or desire, the more effective it will be in preparing. Public announcements and ceremonies focus thought, but the most powerful intensifier of all is prayer or meditation. To be truly effective, thought must be very "vivid in consciousness, definite, steady, sustained, charged with strongly felt good intentions."[78] It must be still but vitally alive, vibrant, just as *dhruva* in the Vedic tradition is a thought that stands still, or *dhāraṇā* in the yogic tradition is a thought that is as still as an oak.

The still point of the Hopi universe is the subjective vibratory axis. Preparing is most intense here, the best place to foster, nurture, and sustain events with maximum power.

How do the Hopi prepare the day? First of all, for them there are no separate days as we speak of them in English. We think of ten days as we would ten different men. If we try to influence the eleventh day, we will be dealing with someone entirely new. For the Hopi, however, there is only one day, a daying, like one man who keeps coming back every morning. If we deal with him properly in the present, he will be influenced in such a way that when he returns he will be friendly. Thus there are no separate days that come one after the other, but only a daying, a process that grows continuously like a plant from the heart of all things.

All events grow from this center, depending upon the intensity of preparation. Eventing is a fluctuating in an energy field. By intense thought the field may be influenced in such a way that the growth of a particular event becomes like a particularly strong area in the field. Strengthening such a field, preparing and sustaining, is brought about by innumerable small, repetitive actions, whether through prayer, dance, or some other form of ritual. To our way of thinking, such repetition is a waste of energy, a diffusion of force into separate moments that will never return. To the Hopi, however, everything is growing, getting later. Not a moment or a movement is lost. Repetitious acts are not wasted but accumulate force. They excite the energy in a field so that it builds and builds. Thus the rain falls from the clouds, prompted by a ceremonial dance consisting of countless staccato dance steps continuing hour after hour. Each step, and each repetition of the chant that goes along with it, is a storing-up of force so that the growth of an event may accelerate. Thus the Hopi think and behave similarly to the way modern physics sees the world, a world in which force is cumulative and can be measured only by acceleration.

Another characteristic of the Hopi world view and language that is somewhat similar to the language of modern physics is the experience of space-time. Suppose that you are singing a song in a Hopi village. Now suppose that someone else were singing a song in the same village, though one hundred years before. In our way of speaking we would say that the two events, the singing of both songs, "took place at the same location."

The Hopi, however, see it differently—more in accordance with Einstein's theory of relativity. For like Einstein, they cannot talk of space without talking of time. For them the song which was sung one hundred years ago is actually in another place, not merely another time. Space-time is not two things but one. All events are space-time events. And since the one-hundred-year-old event happened at a distance in time, it also happened at a distance in space. The past exists far away in space.

But what about events in the very, very distant mythical past? Are they not at a very, very great distance in space? The subjective realm is the inner, vertical, vibratory axis, the heart of all events before they happen. Extending in all directions from this is the objective universe of events. It stretches as far in all directions as an infinite circle surrounding a tree. The Hopi universe is a perpetual growing *away* in time-space from this central axis. As the scientists tell us, when we look out into the galaxies, we are looking into the very distant past.

Far out on the circumference of the Hopi universe are the events that happened in the dim, mythical past. This time-space is so far away that we must, paradoxically, go inward to see it clearly. We can experience it in detail along the vertical subjective axis. In this way the outer limits of the objective universe merge with the inner vertical axis, and with myth. If we wish to know the time-place of the ancient myths we must travel subjectively along this vertical axis. The location on this axis where the time-place of myth is located is just below the surface of the present Earth, or just above. Below our Earth is a land very much like our own, where the Hopi lived in the mythical past. From there, our Earth is their sky. To travel from there to here, one must ascend to and penetrate the dome of their sky, just as the sky of *our* Earth has been penetrated by heroes who find another land, a Heaven, above it. There are several worlds nested one above the other, and the way to travel from one to the next lies within.

The *kiva* is the Hopi's underground ceremonial chamber. Its highest point sticks up above the ground something like an ant-hill. It is in the *kiva* that the Hopi travel to the time-place of myth. Atop the kiva is a hatchway or smoke hole. Through it sticks not a birch tree but a ladder. *Kiva* means, literally, "the world below." A small hole in the floor, below the central fire pit, leads down to the world that the Hopi inhabited before this one. The ladder through the smoke hole leads to the dome of our sky and the land above.

Ill. 42

The Hopi use two labyrinthine symbols to represent the structure of the *kiva*, the Earth, and the human form. The vertical line at the center of the design on the left is the ladder of the *kiva*. It is also the vibratory axis of the earth, and of the human form. It is something like a thread leading through a labyrinth. Spiders, as we all know, can travel quite deftly along an almost invisible vertical thread. And at the opening of the story of the Hopi we found ourselves sitting around the fire in the *kiva*. The flames were being sucked up through the smoke hole toward the galaxies. Inside, Spider Woman was singing the Song of Creation to the First People. Let us enter the *kiva* and travel along the verticle axis, going back to a time-place well below our present Earth, to a time before Spider Woman was created, to Tokpela, the First World.

TOKPELA: THE FIRST WORLD

"The first world was Tokpela [Endless Space].

"But first, they say, there was only the Creator, Taiowa. All else was endless space. There was no beginning and no end, no time, no shape, no life. Just an immeasurable void that had its beginning and end, time, shape, and life in the mind of Taiowa the Creator.

"Then he, the infinite, conceived the finite. First he created Sótuk-nang to make it manifest, saying to him, 'I have created you, the first power and instrument as a person, to carry out my plan for life in endless space. I am your Uncle. You are my Nephew. Go now and lay out these universes in proper order so they may work harmoniously with one another according to my plan.'

"Sótuknang did as he was commanded. From endless space he gathered that which was to be manifest as solid substance, molded it into forms, and arranged them into nine universal kingdoms: one for Taiowa the Creator, one for himself, and seven universes for the life to come. Finishing this, Sótuknang went to Taiowa and asked, 'Is this according to your plan?'

" 'It is very good,' said Taiowa. 'Now I want you to do the same thing with the waters. Place them on the surface of these universes so they will be divided equally among all and each.'

"So Sótuknang gathered from endless space that which was to be manifest as the waters and placed them on the universes so that each would be half solid and half water. Going now to Taiowa, he said, 'I want you to see the work I have done and if it pleases you.'

" 'It is very good,' said Taiowa. 'The next thing now is to put the forces of air into peaceful movement about all.'

"This Sótuknang did. From endless space he gathered that which was to be manifest as the airs, made them into great forces, and arranged them into gentle ordered movements around each universe.

"Taiowa was pleased. 'You have done a great work according to my plan, Nephew. You have created the universes and made them manifest in solids, waters, and winds, and put them in their proper places. But your work is not yet finished. Now you must create life and its movement to complete the four parts, Túwaquachi, of my universal plan.'

SPIDER WOMAN AND THE TWINS

"Sótuknang went to the universe wherein was that to be Tokpela, the First World, and out of it he created her who was to remain on that earth and to be his helper. Her name was Kokyangwuti, Spider Woman.

"When she awoke to life and received her name, she asked, 'Why am I here?'

" 'Look about you,' answered Sótuknang. 'Here is the earth we have created. It has shape and substance, direction and time, a beginning and an end. But there is no life upon it. We see no joyful movement. We hear no joyful sound. What is life without sound and movement? So you have been given the power to help us create this life. You have been given the knowledge, wisdom, and love to bless all the beings you create. That is why you are here.'

"Following his instructions, Spider Woman took some earth, mixed with it some túchvala (liquid from mouth: saliva), and molded it into two beings. Then she covered them with a cape made of white substance which was the creative wisdom itself, and sang the Creation Song over them. When she uncovered them the two beings, twins, sat up and asked, 'Who are we? Why are we here?'

"To the one on the right Spider Woman said, 'You are Pöqánghoya and you are to help keep this world in order when life is put upon it. Go now around all the world and put your hands upon the earth so that it will become fully solidified. This is your duty.'

"Spider Woman said to the twin on the left, 'You are Palönga-whoya and you are to help keep this world in order when life is put upon it. This is your duty now: go about all the world and send out sound so that it may be heard throughout all the land. When this is heard you will also be known as "Echo," for all sound echoes the Creator.'

"Pöqánghoya, traveling throughout the earth, solidified the higher reaches into great mountains. The lower reaches he made firm but still pliable enough to be used by those beings to be placed upon it and who would call it their mother.

"Palöngawhoya, traveling throughout the earth, sounded out his call as he was bidden. All the vibratory centers along the earth's axis from pole to pole resounded his call; the whole earth trembled; the universe quivered in tune. Thus he made the whole world an instrument of sound, and sound an instrument for carrying messages, resounding praise to the Creator of all.

" 'This is your voice, Uncle,' Sótuknang said to Taiowa. 'Everything is tuned to your sound.'

" 'It is very good,' said Taiowa.

"When they had accomplished their duties, Pöqánghoya was sent to the north pole of the world axis and Palöngawhoya to the south pole, where they were jointly commanded to keep the world properly rotating. Pöqánghoya was also given the power to keep the earth in a stable form of solidness. Palöngawhoya was given the power to keep the air in gentle ordered movement, and instructed to send out his call for good or for warning through the vibratory centers of the earth.

" 'These will be your duties in time to come,' said Spider Woman.

"She then created from the earth trees, bushes, plants, flowers, all kinds of seed-bearers and nut-bearers to clothe the earth, giving to each a life and name. In the same manner she created all kinds of birds and animals—molding them out of earth, covering them with her white-substance cape, and singing over them. Some she placed to her right, some to her left, others before and behind her, indicating how they should spread to all four corners of the earth to live.

"Sótuknang was happy, seeing how beautiful it all was—the land, the plants, the birds and animals, and the power working through them all. Joyfully he said to Taiowa, 'Come see what our world looks like now!'

" 'It is very good,' said Taiowa. 'It is ready now for human life, the final touch to complete my plan.'

CREATION OF MANKIND

"So Spider Woman gathered earth, this time of four colors, yellow, red, white, and black; mixed with *túchvala,* the liquid of her mouth; molded them; and covered them with her white-substance cape which was the creative wisdom itself. As before, she sang over them the Creation Song, and when she uncovered them these forms were human beings in the image of Sótuknang. Then she created four other beings after her own form. They were *wúti*, female partners, for the first four male beings.

"When Spider Woman uncovered them the forms came to life. This was at the time of the dark purple light, Qoyangnuptu, the first phase of the dawn of Creation, which first reveals the mystery of man's creation.

"They soon awakened and began to move, but there was still a dampness on their foreheads and a soft spot on their heads. This was at the time of the yellow light, Síkangnuqua, the second phase of the dawn of Creation, when the breath of life entered man.

"In a short time the sun appeared above the horizon, drying the dampness on their foreheads and hardening the soft spot on their heads. This was the time of the red light, Tálawva, the third phase of the dawn of Creation, when man, fully formed and firmed, proudly faced his Creator.

" 'That is the Sun,' said Spider Woman. 'You are meeting your Father the Creator for the first time. You must always remember and observe these three phases of your Creation. The time of the three lights, the dark purple, the yellow, and the red, reveal in turn the mystery, the breath of life, and warmth of love. These comprise the Creator's plan of life for you as sung over you in the Song of Creation' [which she then sang to them].

"The First People of the First World did not answer her; they could not speak. Something had to be done. Since Spider Woman received her power from Sótuknang, she had to call him and ask him what to do. So she called Palöngawhoya and said, 'Call your Uncle. We need him at once.'

"Palöngahoya, the echo twin, sent out his call along the world axis to the vibratory centers of the earth, which resounded his message throughout the universe. 'Sótuknang, our Uncle, come at once! We need you!'

"All at once, with the sound as of a mighty wind, Sótuknang appeared in front of them. 'I am here. Why do you need me so urgently?'

Spider Woman explained, 'As you commanded me, I have created these First People. They are fully and firmly formed; they are properly colored; they have life; they have movement. But they cannot talk. That is the proper thing they lack. So I want you to give them speech. Also the wisdom and the power to reproduce, so that they may enjoy their life and give thanks to the Creator.'

"So Sótuknang gave them speech, a different language to each color, with respect for each other's difference. He gave them the wisdom and the power to reproduce and multiply.

"Then he said to them, 'With all these I have given you this world to live on and to be happy. There is only one thing I ask of you. To respect the Creator at all times. Wisdom, harmony, and respect for the love of the Creator who made you. May it grow and never be forgotten among you as long as you live.'

"So the First People went their directions, were happy, and began to multiply.

THE NATURE OF MAN

"With the pristine wisdom granted them, they understood that the earth was a living entity like themselves. She was their mother; they were made from her flesh; they suckled at her breast. For her milk was the grass upon which all animals grazed and the corn which had been created specially to supply food for mankind. But the corn plant was also a living entity with a body similar to man's in many respects, and the people built its flesh into their own. Hence corn was also their mother. Thus they knew their mother in two aspects which were often synonymous—as Mother Earth and the Corn Mother.

"In their wisdom they also knew their father in two aspects. He was the Sun, the solar god of their universe. Not until he first appeared to them at the time of the red light, Tálawva, had they been fully firmed and formed. Yet his was but the face through which looked Taiowa, their Creator.

"These universal entities were their real parents, their human parents being but the instruments through which their power was made manifest. In modern times their descendants remembered this.

"When a child was born his Corn Mother was placed beside him, where it was kept for twenty days, and during this period he was kept in darkness; for while his newborn body was of this world, he was still under the protection of his universal parents. If the child was born at night, four lines were painted with cornmeal on each of the four walls and ceiling early next morning. If he was born during the day, the lines were painted the following morning. The lines signified that a spiritual home, as well as a temporal home, had been prepared for him on earth.

"On the first day the child was washed with water in which cedar had been brewed. Fine white cornmeal was then rubbed over his body and left all day. Next day the child was cleaned, and cedar ashes were rubbed over him to remove the hair and baby skin. This was repeated for three days. From the fifth day until the twentieth day, he was washed and rubbed with cornmeal for one day and covered with ashes for four days. Meanwhile the child's mother drank a little of the cedar water each day.

"On the fifth day the hair of both child and mother was washed, and one cornmeal line was scraped off each wall and ceiling. The scrapings were then taken to the shrine where the umbilical cord had been deposited. Each fifth day thereafter another line of cornmeal was removed from walls and ceiling and taken to the shrine.

"For nineteen days now the house had been kept in darkness so that the child had not seen any light. Early on the morning of the twentieth day, while it was still dark, all the aunts of the child arrived at the house, each carrying a Corn Mother in her right hand and each wishing to be the child's godmother. First the child was bathed. Then the mother, holding the child in her left arm, took up the Corn Mother that had lain beside the child and passed it over the child four times from the navel upward to the head. On the first pass she named the child; on the second she wished the child a long life; on the third, a healthy life. If the child was a boy she wished him a productive life in his work on the fourth pass; if a girl, that she would become a good wife and mother.

"Each of the aunts in turn did likewise, giving the child a name from the clan of either the mother or father of the aunt. The child was then given back to its mother. The yellow light by then was showing in the east. The mother, holding the child in her left arm and the Corn Mother in her right hand, and accompanied by her own mother—the child's grandmother—left the house and walked toward the east. Then they stopped, facing east, and prayed silently, casting pinches of cornmeal toward the rising sun.

"When the sun cleared the horizon the mother stepped forward, held up the child to the sun, and said, 'Father Sun, this is your child.' Again she said this, passing the Corn Mother over the child's body as when she had named him, wishing for him to grow so old he would have to lean on a crook for support, thus proving that he obeyed the Creator's laws. The grandmother did the same thing when the mother had finished. Then both marked a cornmeal path toward the sun for this new life.

"The child now belonged to his family and the earth. Mother and grandmother carried him back to the house, where his aunts were waiting. The village crier announced his birth, and a feast was held in his honor. For several years the child was called by the different names that were given him. The one that seemed most predominant became his name, and the aunt who gave it to him became his godmother. The Corn Mother remained his spiritual mother.

"For seven or eight years he led the normal earthly life of a child. Then came his first initiation into a religious society, and he began to learn that, although he had human parents, his real parents were the universal entities who had created him through them—his Mother Earth, from whose flesh all are born, and his Father Sun, the solar god who gives life to all the universe. He began to learn, in brief, that he too had two aspects. He was a member of an earthly family and tribal clan, and he was a citizen of the great universe, to which he owed a growing allegiance as his understanding developed.

"The First People, then, understood the mystery of their parenthood. In their pristine wisdom they also understood their own structure and functions—the nature of man himself.

"The living body of man and the living body of the earth were constructed in the same way. Through each ran an axis, man's axis being the backbone, the vertebral column, which controlled the equilibrium of his movements and his functions. Along this axis were several vibratory centers which echoed the primordial sound of life throughout the universe or sounded a warning if anything went wrong.

"The first of these in man lay at the top of the head. Here when he was born, was the soft spot, *kópavi*, the 'open door' through which he received his life and communicated with his Creator. For with every breath the soft spot moved up and down with a gentle vibration that was communicated to the Creator. At the time of the red light, Tálawva, the last phase of his creation, the soft spot was hardened and the door was closed. It remained closed until his death; opening then for his life to depart as it had come.

"Just below it lay the second center, the organ that man learned to think with by himself, the thinking organ called the brain. Its earthly function enabled man to think about his actions and work on this earth.

But the more he understood that his work and actions should conform
to the plan of the Creator, the more clearly he understood that the real
function of the thinking organ called the brain was carrying out the plan
of all Creation.

"The third center lay in the throat. It tied together those openings
in his nose and mouth through which he received the breath of life and
the vibratory organs that enabled him to give back his breath in sound.
This primordial sound, as that coming from the vibratory centers of the
body of earth, was attuned to the universal vibration of all Creation.
New and diverse sounds were given forth by these vocal organs in the
forms of speech and song, their secondary function for man on this
earth. But as he came to understand its primary function, he used this
center to speak and sing praises to the Creator.

"The fourth center was the heart. It too was a vibrating organ,
pulsing with the vibration of life itself. In his heart man felt the good
of life, its sincere purpose. He was of One Heart. But there were those
who permitted evil feelings to enter. They were said to be of Two
Hearts.

"The last of man's important centers lay under his navel, the organ
some people now call the solar plexus. As this name signifies, it was the
throne in man of the Creator himself. From it he directed all the
functions of man.

"The first People knew no sickness. Not until evil entered the world
did persons get sick in the body or head. It was then that a medicine
man, knowing how man was constructed, could tell what was wrong with
a person by examining these centers. First, he laid his hands on them:
the top of the head, above the eyes, the throat, the chest, the belly. The
hands of the medicine man were seer instruments; they could feel the
vibrations from each center and tell him in which life ran strongest or
weakest. Sometimes the trouble was just a bellyache from uncooked food
or a cold in the head. But other times it came 'from outside,' drawn by
the person's own evil thoughts, or from those of a Two Hearts. In this
case the medicine man took out from his medicine pouch a small crystal
about an inch and a half across, held it in the sun to get it in working
order, and then looked through it at each of the centers. In this manner
he could see what caused the trouble and often the very face of the Two
Hearts person who had caused the illness. There was nothing magical
about the crystal, medicine men always said. An ordinary person could
see nothing when he looked through it; the crystal merely objectified the

vision of the center which controlled his eyes and which the medicine man had developed for this very purpose. . . .

"Thus the First People understood themselves. And this was the First World they lived upon. Its name was Tokpela, Endless Space. Its direction was west; its color *sikyangpu,* yellow; its mineral *sikyásvu,* gold. Significant upon it were *káto'ya,* the snake with a big head; *wisoko,* the fat-eating bird; and *muha,* the little four-leaved plant. On it the First People were pure and happy.

TOKPA: THE SECOND WORLD

"So the First People kept multiplying and spreading over the face of the land and were happy. Although they were of different colors and spoke different languages, they felt as one and understood one another without talking. It was the same with the birds and animals. They all suckled at the breast of their Mother Earth, who gave them her milk of grass, seeds, fruit, and corn, and they all felt as one, people and animals.

"But gradually there were those who forgot the commands of Sótuknang and the Spider Woman to respect their Creator. More and more they used the vibratory centers of their bodies solely for earthly purposes, forgetting that their primary purpose was to carry out the plan of Creation.

"There then came among them Lavaíhoya, the Talker. He came in the form of a bird called Mochni [bird like a mocking bird], and the more he kept talking the more he convinced them of the differences between them: the difference between people and animals, and the differences between the people themselves by reason of the colors of their skins, their speech, and belief in the plan of the Creator.

"It was then that animals drew away from people. The guardian spirit of animals laid his hands on their hind legs just below the tail, making them become wild and scatter from the people in fear. You can see this slightly oily spot today on deer and antelope—on the sides of their back legs as they throw up their tails to run away.

"In the same way, people began to divide and draw away from one another—those of different races and languages, then those who remembered the plan of Creation and those who did not.

"There came among them a handsome one, Káto'ya, in the form of a snake with a big head. He led the people still farther away from one another and their pristine wisdom. They became suspicious of one another and accused one another wrongfully until they became fierce and warlike and began to fight one another.

"All the time Mochni kept talking and Káto'ya became more beguiling. There was no rest, no peace.

"But among all the people of different races and languages there were a few in every group who still lived by the laws of Creation. To them came Sótuknang. He came with the sound as of a mighty wind and suddenly appeared before them. He said, 'I have observed this state of affairs. It is not good. It is so bad I talked to my Uncle, Taiowa, about it. We have decided this world must be destroyed and another one created so you people can start over again. You are the ones we have chosen.'

"They listened carefully to their instructions.

"Said Sótuknang, 'You will go to a certain place. Your kópavi [vibratory center on top of the head] will lead you. This inner wisdom will give you the sight to see a certain cloud, which you will follow by day, and a certain star, which you will follow by night. Take nothing with you. Your journey will not end until the cloud stops and the star stops.'

"So all over the world these chosen people suddenly disappeared from their homes and people and began following the cloud by day and the star by night. Many other people asked them where they were going and when they were told laughed at them. "We don't see any cloud or any star either!" they said. This was because they had lost the inner vision of the kópavi on the crown of their head; the door was closed to them. Still there were a very few who went along anyway because they believed the people who did see the cloud and the star. This was all right.

"After many days and nights the first people arrived at the certain place. Soon others came and asked, 'What are you doing here?' And they said, 'We were told by Sótuknang to come here.' The other people said, 'We too were led here by the vapor and the star!' They were all happy together because they were of the same mind and understanding even though they were of different races and languages.

"When the last ones arrived Sótuknang appeared. 'Well, you are all here, you people I have chosen to save from the destruction of this world. Now come with me.'

"He led them to a big mound where the Ant People lived, stamped on the roof, and commanded the Ant People to open up their home. When an opening was made on the top of the anthill, Sótuknang said to the people, 'Now you will enter this Ant kiva, where you will be safe when I destroy the world. While you are here I want you to learn a lesson from these Ant People. They are industrious. They gather food in the summer for the winter. They keep cool when it is hot and warm when it is cool. They live peacefully with one another. They obey the plan of Creation.'

"So the people went down to live with the Ant People. When they were all safe and settled Taiowa commanded Sótuknang to destroy the world. Sótuknang destroyed it by fire because the Fire Clan had been its leaders. He rained fire upon it. He opened up the volcanoes. Fire came from above and below and all around until the earth, the waters, the air, all was one element, fire, and there was nothing left except the people safe inside the womb of the earth.

"This was the end of Tokpela, the First World.

EMERGENCE TO THE SECOND WORLD

"While this was going on the people lived happily underground with the Ant People. Their homes were just like the people's homes on the earth-surface being destroyed. There were rooms to live in and rooms where they stored their food. There was light to see by, too. The tiny bits of crystal in the sand of the anthill had absorbed the light of the sun, and by using the inner vision of the center behind their eyes they could see by its reflection very well.

"Only one thing troubled them. The food began to run short. It had not taken Sótuknang long to destroy the world, nor would it take him long to create another one. But it was taking a long time for the First World to cool off before the Second World could be created. That was why the food was running short.

" 'Do not give us so much of the food you have worked so hard to gather and store,' the people said.

" 'Yes, you are our guests,' the Ant People told them. 'What we have is yours also.' So the Ant People continued to deprive themselves of food in order to supply their guests. Every day they tied their belts tighter and tighter. That is why ants today are so small around the waist.

"Finally that which had been the First World cooled off. Sótuknang purified it. Then he began to create the Second World. He changed its form completely, putting land where the water was and water where the land had been, so the people upon their Emergence would have nothing to remind them of the previous wicked world.

"When all was ready he came to the roof of the Ant kiva, stamped on it, and gave his call. Immediately the Chief of the Ant People went up to the opening and rolled back the *núta*. '*Yung-ai!* Come in! You are welcome!' he called.

"Sótuknang spoke first to the Ant People. 'I am thanking you for doing your part in helping to save these people. It will always be remembered, this you have done. The time will come when another world will be destroyed; and when wicked people know their last day on earth has come, they will sit by an anthill and cry for the ants to save them. Now, having fulfilled your duty, you may go forth to this Second World I have created and take your place as ants.'

"Then Sótuknang said to the people, 'Make your Emergence now to this Second World I have created. It is not quite so beautiful as the First World, but it is beautiful just the same. You will like it. So multiply and be happy. But remember your Creator and the laws he gave you. When I hear you singing joyful praises to him I will know you are my children, and you will be close to me in your hearts.'

"So the people emerged to the Second World. Its name was Tokpa [Dark Midnight]. Its direction was south, its color blue, its mineral *qöchásiva*, silver. Chiefs upon it were *salavi*, the spruce; *kwáhu*, the eagle; and *kolíchiyaw*, the skunk.

"It was a big land, and the people multiplied rapidly, spreading over it to all directions, even to the other side of the world. This did not matter, for they were so close together in spirit they could see and talk to each other from the center on top of the head. Because this door was still open, they felt close to Sótuknang and they sang joyful praises to the Creator, Taiowa.

"They did not have the privilege of living with the animals, though, for the animals were wild and kept apart. Being separated from the animals, the people tended to their own affairs. They built homes, then villages and trails between them. They made things with their hands and stored food like the Ant People. Then they began to trade and barter with one another.

"This was when the trouble started. Everything they needed was on this Second World, but they began to want more. More and more they traded for things they didn't need, and the more goods they got, the more they wanted. This was very serious. For they did not realize they were drawing away, step by step, from the good life given them. They just forgot to sing joyful praises to the Creator and soon began to sing praises for the goods they bartered and stored. Before long it happened as it had to happen. The people began to quarrel and fight, and then wars between villages began.

"Still there were a few people in every village who sang the song of their Creation. But the wicked people laughed at them until they could sing it only in their hearts. Even so, Sótuknang heard it through their centers and the centers of the earth. Suddenly one day he appeared before them.

" 'Spider Woman tells me your thread is running out on this world,' he said. 'That is too bad. The Spider Clan was your leader, and you were making good progress until this state of affairs began. Now my Uncle, Taiowa, and I have decided we must do something about it. We are going to destroy this Second World just as soon as we put you people who still have the song in your hearts in a safe place.'

"So again, as on the First World, Sótuknang called on the Ant People to open up their underground world for the chosen people. When they were safely underground, Sótuknang commanded the twins, Pöqánghoya and Palöngawhoya, to leave their posts at the north and south ends of the world axis where they were stationed to keep the earth properly rotating.

"The twins had hardly abandoned their stations when the world, with no one to control it, teetered off balance, spun around crazily, then rolled over twice. Mountains plunged into seas with a great splash, seas and lakes sloshed over the land; and as the world spun through cold and lifeless space it froze into solid ice.

"This was the end of Tokpa, the Second World.

EMERGENCE TO THE THIRD WORLD

"For many years all the elements that had comprised the Second World were frozen into a motionless and lifeless lump of ice. But the people were happy and warm with the Ant People in their underground world. They watched their food carefully, although the ants' waists became still smaller. They wove sashes and blankets together and told stories.

"Eventually Sótuknang ordered Pöqánghoya and Palöngawhoya back to their stations at the poles of the world axis. With a great shudder and a splintering of ice the planet began rotating again. When it was revolving smoothly about its own axis and stately moving in its universal orbit, the ice began to melt and the world began to warm to life. Sótuknang set about creating the Third World: arranging earths and seas, planting mountains and plains with their proper coverings and creating all forms of life.

"When the earth was ready for occupancy, he came to the Ant kiva with the proper approach as before and said, 'Open the door. It is time for you to come out.'

"Once again when the *núta* was rolled back he gave the people their instructions. 'I have saved you so you can be planted again on this new Third World. But you must always remember the two things I am saying to you now. First, respect me and one another. And second, sing in harmony from the tops of the hills. When I do not hear you singing praises to your Creator I will know you have gone back to evil again.'

"So the people climbed up the ladder from the Ant kiva, making their Emergence to the Third World.

KUSKURZA: THE THIRD WORLD

"Its name was Kuskurza, its direction east, its color red. Chiefs upon it were the mineral *palásiva*, copper; the plant *píva*, tobacco; the bird *angwusi*, crow; and the animal *chöövio*, antelope.

"Upon it once more the people spread out, multiplied, and continued their progress on the Road of Life. In the First World they had lived simply with the animals. In the Second World they had developed handicrafts, homes, and villages. Now in the Third World they multiplied in such numbers and advanced so rapidly that they created big cities, countries, a whole civilization. This made it difficult for them to conform to the plan of Creation and to sing praises to Taiowa and Sótuknang. More and more of them became wholly occupied with their own earthly plans.

"Some of them, of course, retained the wisdom granted them upon their Emergence. With this wisdom they understood that the farther they proceeded on the Road of Life and the more they developed, the harder it was. That was why their world was destroyed every so often to give them a fresh start. They were especially concerned because so many people were using their reproductive power in wicked ways. There was one woman who was becoming known throughout the world for her wickedness in corrupting so many people. She even boasted that so many men were giving her turquoise necklaces for her favors she could wind them around a ladder that reached to the end of the world's axis. So the people with wisdom sang louder and longer their praises to the Creator from the tops of their hills.

"The other people hardly heard them. Under the leadership of the Bow Clan they began to use their creative power in another evil and destructive way. Perhaps this was caused by that wicked woman. But some of them made a *pátuwvota* [shield made of hide] and with their creative power made it fly through the air. On this many of the people flew to a big city, attacked it, and returned so fast no one knew where they came from. Soon the people of many cities and countries were making *pátuwvotas* and flying on them to attack one another. So corruption and war came to the Third World as it had to the others.

"This time Sótuknang came to Spider Woman and said, 'There is no use waiting until the thread runs out this time. Something has to be done lest the people with the song in their hearts are corrupted and killed off too. It will be difficult with all this destruction going on for them to gather at the far end of the world I have designated. But I will help them. Then you will save them when I destroy this world with water.'

" 'How shall I save them?' asked Spider Woman.

" 'When you get there look about you,' commanded Sótuknang. 'You will see these tall plants with hollow stems. Cut them down and put the people inside. Then I will tell you what to do next.'

"Spider Woman did as he instructed her. She cut down the hollow reeds; and as the people came to her, she put them inside with a little water and *hurúsuki* (white cornmeal dough) for food, and sealed them up. When all the people were thus taken care of, Sótuknang appeared.

" 'Now you get in to take care of them, and I will seal you up,' he said. 'Then I will destroy the world.'

"So he loosed the waters upon the earth. Waves higher than mountains rolled in upon the land. Continents broke asunder and sank beneath the seas. And still the rains fell, the waves rolled in.

"The people sealed in their hollow reeds heard the mighty rushing of the waters. They felt themselves tossed high in the air and dropping back to the water. Then all was quiet, and they knew they were floating. For a long, long time—so long a time that it seemed it would never end —they kept floating.

"Finally their movement ceased. The Spider Woman unsealed their hollow reeds, took them by the tops of their heads, and pulled them out. 'Bring out all the food that is left over,' she commanded.

"The people brought out *hurúsuki;* it was still the same size, although they had been eating it all this time. Looking about them, they saw they were on a little piece of land that had been the top of one of their highest mountains. All else, as far as they could see, was water. This was all that remained of the Third World.

" 'There must be some dry land somewhere we can go to,' they said. 'Where is the new Fourth World that Sótuknang has created for us?' They sent many kinds of birds, one after another, to fly over the waters and find it. But they all came back tired out without having seen any sign of land. Next they planted a reed that grew high into the sky. Up it they climbed and stared over the surface of the waters. But they saw no sign of land.

"Then Sótuknang appeared to Spider Woman and said, 'You must continue traveling on. Your inner wisdom will guide you. The door at the top of your head is open.'

"So Spider Woman directed the people to make round, flat boats of the hollow reeds they had come in and to crawl inside. Again they entrusted themselves to the water and the inner wisdom to guide them. For a long time they drifted with the wind and the movement of the waters and came to another rocky island.

" 'It is bigger than the other one, but it is not big enough,' they said, looking around them and thinking they heard a low rumbling noise.

" 'No. It is not big enough,' said Spider Woman.

"So the people kept traveling toward the rising sun in their reed boats. After awhile they said, 'There is that low rumbling noise we heard. We must be coming to land again.'

"So it was. A big land, it seemed, with grass and trees and flowers beautiful to their weary eyes. On it they rested a long time. Some of the people wanted to stay, but Spider Woman said, 'No. It is not the place. You must continue on.'

"Leaving their boats, they traveled by foot eastward across the island to the water's edge. Here they found growing some more of the hollow plants like reeds or bamboo, which they cut down. Directed by Spider Woman, they laid some of these in a row with another row on top of them in the opposite direction and tied them all together with vines and leaves. This made a raft big enough for one family or more. When enough rafts were made for all, Spider Woman directed them to make paddles.

" 'You will be going uphill from now on and you will have to make your own way. So Sótuknang told you: The farther you go, the harder it gets.'

"After long and weary traveling, still east and a little north, the people began to hear the low rumbling noise and saw land. One family and clan after another landed with joy. The land was long, wide, and beautiful. The earth was rich and flat, covered with trees and plants, seed-bearers and nut-bearers, providing lots of food. The people were happy and kept staying there year after year.

" 'No. This is not the Fourth World,' Spider Woman kept telling them. 'It is too easy and pleasant for you to live on, and you would soon fall into evil ways again. You must go on. Have we not told you the way becomes harder and longer?'

"Reluctantly the people traveled eastward by foot across the island to the far shore. Again they made rafts and paddles. When they were ready to set forth Spider Woman said, 'Now I have done all I am commanded to do for you. You must go on alone and find your own place of Emergence. Just keep your doors open, and your spirits will guide you.'

" 'Thank you, Spider Woman, for all you have done for us,' they said sadly. 'We will remember what you have said.'

"Alone they set out, traveling east and a little north, paddling hard day and night for many days as if they were paddling uphill.

"At last they saw land. It rose high above the waters, stretching from north to south as far as they could see. A great land, a mighty land, their inner wisdom told them. 'The Fourth World!' they cried to each other.

"As they got closer, its shores rose higher and higher into a steep wall of mountains. There seemed no place to land. 'Let us go north. There we will find our Place of Emergence,' said some. So they went north, but the mountains rose higher and steeper.

" 'No! Let us go south! There we will find our Place of Emergence!' cried others. So they turned south and traveled many days more. But here too the mountain wall reared higher.

"Not knowing what to do, the people stopped paddling, opened the doors on top of their heads, and let themselves be guided. Almost immediately the water smoothed out, and they felt their rafts caught up in a gentle current. Before long they landed and joyfully jumped out upon a sandy shore. 'The Fourth World!' they cried. 'We have reached our Place of Emergence at last!'

"Soon all the others arrived and when they were gathered together Sótuknang appeared before them. 'Well, I see you are all here. That is good. This is the place I have prepared for you. Look now at the way you have come.'

"Looking to the west and the south, the people could see sticking out of the water the islands upon which they had rested.

" 'They are the footprints of your journey,' continued Sótuknang, 'the tops of the high mountains of the Third World, which I destroyed. Now watch.'

"As the people watched them, the closest one sank under the water, then the next, until all were gone, and they could see only water.

" 'See,' said Sótuknang, 'I have washed away even the footprints of your Emergence; the stepping-stones which I left for you. Down on the bottom of the seas lie all the proud cities, the flying *pátuwvotas,* and the worldly treasures corrupted with evil, and those people who found no time to sing praises to the Creator from the tops of their hills. But the day will come, if you preserve the memory and the meaning of your Emergence, when these stepping-stones will emerge again to prove the truth you speak.'

"This at last was the end of the Third World, Kuskurza [an ancient name for which there is no modern meaning].

Túwaqachi: The Fourth World

" 'I have something more to say before I leave you,' Sótuknang told the people as they stood at their Place of Emergence on the shore of the present Fourth World. This is what he said:

" 'The name of this Fourth World is Túwaqachi, World Complete. You will find out why. It is not all beautiful and easy like the previous ones. It has height and depth, heat and cold, beauty and barrenness; it has everything for you to choose from. What you choose will determine if this time you can carry out the plan of Creation on it or whether it must in time be destroyed too. Now you will separate and go different ways to claim all the earth for the Creator. Each group of you will follow your own star until it stops. There you will settle. Now I must go. But you will have help from the proper deities, from your good spirits. Just keep your own doors open and always remember what I have told you. This is what I say.'

"Then he disappeared.

"The people began to move slowly off the shore and into the land, when they heard the low rumbling noise again. Looking around, they saw a handsome man and asked, 'Are you the one who has been making these noises we have heard?'

" 'Yes. I made them to help you find the way here. Do you not recognize me? My name is Másaw. I am the caretaker, the guardian and protector of this land.'

"The people recognized Másaw. He had been appointed head caretaker of the Third World, but, becoming a little self-important, he had lost his humility before the Creator. Being a spirit, he could not die, so Taiowa took his appointment away from him and made him the deity of death and the underworld. This job Below was not as pleasant as the one Above. Then when the Third World was destroyed, Taiowa decided to give him another chance, as he had the people, and appointed him to guard and protect this Fourth World as its caretaker.

"He was the first being the people had met here, and they were very respectful to him. 'Will you give us your permission to live on this land?' they asked.

" 'Yes, I will give you my permission as owner of the land.'

" 'Will you be our leader?' the people then asked.

" 'No,' replied Másaw. 'A greater one than I has given you a plan to fulfill first. When the previous parts of the world were pushed underneath the water, this new land was pushed up in the middle to become the backbone of the earth. You are now standing on its *átvila* [west side slope]. But you have not yet made your migrations. You have not yet followed your stars to the place where you will meet and settle. This you must do before I can become your leader. But if you go back to evil ways again I will take over the earth from you, for I am its caretaker, guardian, and protector. To the north you will find cold and ice. That is the Back Door to this land, and those who may come through this Back Door will enter without my consent. So go now and claim the land with my permission.'

"When Másaw disappeared, the people divided into groups and clans to begin their migrations.

" 'May we meet again!' they all called back to one another.

"This is how it all began on this, our present Fourth World. As we know, its name is Túwaqachi, World Complete, its direction north, its color *sikyangpu*, yellowish white. Chiefs upon it are the tree *kneumapee*, juniper; the bird *mongwau*, the owl; the animal *tohopko*, the mountain lion; and the mixed mineral *sikyápala*.

"Where all the people went on their migrations to the ends of the earth and back, and what they have done to carry out the plan of Creation from this Place of Beginning to the present time, is to be told next by all the clans as they came in."[79]

Ill. 43

Cante Hondo

Music heard so deeply
That it is not heard at all, but you are the music
While the music lasts.

—T. S. ELIOT

The Word is the tree planted by the water's edge which the Father
has begotten without intermediary, laden with fruit, flourishing, tall,
fair-branched. . . . It was of this tree that Adam refused the fruit and
fell victim to its opposite. Christ is the tree of life, the devil the tree
of death.

—ASTERIUS THE SOPHIST

Before the coming of the white man and the disappearance of the buffalo, the Blackfoot Indians of Montana were a hunting tribe that depended for sustenance on the great herds that roamed the prairies. The buffalo were lured toward a cliff by a man dressed in buffalo hide and a buffalo headdress. Meanwhile other Blackfeet frightened the animals in the rear of the herd until they stampeded, pushing the entire herd over the precipice to its death.

One year, as a Blackfoot legend tells it, things did not go so smoothly. The buffalo were led up to the cliff, but they would not jump. They merely swerved to the right or the left, escaping onto the prairie. The Blackfeet were without meat and near the point of starvation.

And so it was that a young woman of the tribe, as she went to fetch water in the early dawn, saw an entire herd of buffalo grazing on the prairie just above the cliff. Half in jest she cried out, "If you will only jump over the cliff, I will marry one of you!" And right before her eyes they stumbled and fell to their death. Only one big bull buffalo survived. And he approached the beautiful young squaw saying, "Come with me!"

"No, no," she protested, trying to escape.

But he reminded her that she had promised to marry one of them if they would only jump. And so she became the buffalo's bride and was led off onto the prairie.

Now when the tribe had finished skinning the buffalo and cutting up the meat, they could not find the young woman. Her father, taking his bow and arrows, set out onto the great prairie to find her.

After traveling a long distance he came upon a buffalo wallow—a watering hole where the herds come to drink and roll in the mud. In the distance he saw a herd, but being fatigued from his journey he sat down wondering what he should do. As he thought, a lovely black and white bird, a magpie, alighted on the ground near him.

The father said to the bird, "Help me if you can. You have wings and can fly swiftly around. Look for my daughter, and if you see her, tell her that her father is near the wallow."

The magpie flew to the herd and saw the young woman. He landed on the ground near to where she sat and said, "Your father is waiting for you at the wallow."

"Don't speak so loudly," cautioned the young woman. "My buffalo husband is sleeping nearby. Fly back and tell my father to wait."

Soon the great bull awoke and was thirsty. He said to his wife, "Go and fetch me some water."

The young woman was delighted at these words and, taking a horn from the buffalo's head, went to the wallow. When she arrived there she warned her father, "You should not have come. They will kill you!"

"I have come to take you home," he replied. "Hurry, let's go!"

"No, not now!" she cried. "They will chase and kill us. Wait until they are asleep, and then we will sneak away."

She returned to the great bull with the horn full of water. He drank some and then shouted, "There is someone at the wallow!" He began to bellow and snort and dig at the dirt with his sharp black hooves. All the bulls leaped up tossing their horns, bellowing loudly, and rushed toward the wallow. When they found the man they trampled him, and then tore at him with their horns, and then trampled him again until nothing was left.

The girl wailed, "Oh, Father, Father!" and sank to the ground in tears.

"Aha!" bellowed the great bull. "You are crying because your father is dead. Perhaps now you will know how we feel. We have seen our fathers, mothers, sisters, brothers, and many other dear ones slaughtered by your tribe. And so I pity you. If you can bring your father back to life, I will allow both of you to return to your tribe."

The young woman then saw the magpie and pleaded, "Help me, please! Try to find one of my father's bones."

The magpie searched and pecked all through the mud, and finally found a joint of the backbone. He gave this to the young woman.

She put the bone on the ground, covered it with her robe, and chanted a magic song. When she removed the robe, her father's entire body was lying there, though dead. She covered the body with her robe and chanted the song again. When she removed the robe the second time her father was breathing, and stood up. The buffalo were astonished and the magpie was delighted.

"You have brought your father back from the dead," said the bull. "Your holy power is very great. Before you both leave, we will teach you our dance and song. You must remember these. For by means of them, the buffalo killed by your tribe will be restored to life."

Then the entire herd danced and sang the solemn buffalo dance and the father and his daughter were attentive. When they returned to their tribe, they taught what they had learned.[80]

Now resurrection from bones, and from the Word, is a widespread theme among hunting and nomadic tribes all over the world. The shamans of Siberia, for instance, as part of their initiation, often have a dream or vision of being reduced to a skeleton. In the dream or vision the spirits of departed shamans come and eat away the flesh until only the white bones remain, glowing with supernal light. The young initiate is then reborn as a shaman and is no longer afraid of death. In Tibetan Buddhism and even in Christianity monks practice a contemplation in which they reduce themselves mentally to the condition of a skeleton in order to experience the illusory quality of life. For both the Buddhists and the Christians, there is a scriptural basis for the practice. The biblical account appears in Ezekiel's famous vision:

The hand of the Lord was upon me, and carried me out in the spirit of the Lord, and set me down in the midst of a valley which was full of bones. . . . And he said unto me, Son of man, can these bones live? And I answered, O Lord God, thou knowest. Again he said unto me, Prophesy upon these bones, and say unto them, O ye dry bones, hear the word of the Lord. Thus saith the Lord God unto these bones; Behold, I will cause breath to enter into you, and ye shall live: . . . and ye shall know that I am the Lord. So I prophesied as I was commanded: and as I prophesied, there was a noise, and behold a shaking, and the bones came together, bone to his bone. And when I beheld, lo, the sinews and the flesh came up upon them. . . .[81]

In this same way T. S. Eliot, the greatest metaphysical poet of the twentieth century to deal with Christianity, finds his bones scattered about the desert, and his flesh eaten away by leopards.

Lady, three white leopards sat under a juniper-tree
In the cool of the day, having fed to satiety
On my legs my heart my liver and that which had been contained
In the hollow round of my skull.[82]

His scattered bones present, to say the least, a highly fragmented image, signifying a state of dissolution of the personality—the ruins of the shattered self. Yet like the incantations of the Blackfoot girl chanting over her father's backbone, like Ezekiel prophesying over an entire valley of bones, and like the entire Blackfoot tribe dancing and chanting the buffalo dance, the Word brings a new center and new life for Eliot.

That Eliot's *The Waste Land* appeared immediately following World War I is of the greatest importance. For the fragmentation of which he wrote in that poem was not only his own, but that of the entire society. The songs Eliot sang later were like the songs taught to the Blackfoot Indians. They could resurrect the soul of an individual or an entire society.

And there appeared at that time after the nations had fruitlessly pitted their strength against one another, strewing the battlefields with bones, a common vision. From the scattered remains of the family of nations a new center emerged. The great Western sages arose from their hermitages to proclaim the power of symbols, and especially the power of symbols to effect the reintegration of individual personalities and entire societies. From his hermitage in the Swiss Alps, the psychologist Carl Jung spoke of the symbol of the *maṇḍala* and its basic function:

the premonition of a center of personality, a kind of central point within the psyche, to which everything is related, by which everything is arranged, and which is itself a source of energy. . . . This center is not felt or thought of as the ego, but if one may so express it, as the *self.* Although the center is represented by an innermost point, it is surrounded by a periphery containing everything that belongs to the self— the paired opposites that make up the total personality. This totality comprises consciousness first of all, then the personal unconscious, and finally an indefinitely large segment of the collective unconscious whose archetypes are common to all mankind.[83]

T. S. Eliot's *The Waste Land* was also drafted in Switzerland, during a rest cure at Lausanne in 1921, a time when the poet was deeply concerned with the wasteland of postwar Europe. The poem itself is an incoherent stream of broken images, strewn like scattered bones to create an effect of psychological and social disintegration.

And yet there is, near the end of the poem, a flash of illumination, a foretelling, an emergent pattern. For a brief moment the skies open and we hear the voice of the Lord of All Creatures thundering a single, simple syllable, DA. It is a single command—a still point around which, as we have seen, the ego-transcending activities of giving, being compassionate, and being self-controlled move. Among the scattered bones—the disassembled ruins of a personality and postwar Europe—a new center emerges; the still point in the form of the Word thunders, and is gone.

The aim of life, for Eliot, is to move toward that center and somehow gain permanent union with it.

We must be still and still moving
Into another intensity
For a further union, a deeper communion.[84]

But this vision of ecstasy and illumination, the still point, is too intense for humankind to bear. The silent heart of light comes only in flashes. Only saints really know the still point.

For most of us, there is only the unattended
Moment, the moment in and out of time,
The distraction fit, lost in a shaft of sunlight,
The wild thyme unseen, or the winter lightning
Or the waterfall, or music heard so deeply
That it is not heard at all, but you are the music
While the music lasts. These are only hints and guesses,
Hints followed by guesses.[85]

We have only clues, hints, distracted moments, intimations of the unmoving center of

The inner freedom from the practical desire,
The release from action and suffering, release from the inner
And outer compulsion, yet surrounded
By a grace of sense, a white light still and moving.[86]

This luminous Word at the center of the world is the focal point of a *mandala* or *yantra* that comes to fruition in the poet's monumental work *Four Quartets*. As we know, the *maṇḍala* usually contains three elements: the central point, the circle, and the idea of fourness. In the very name *Four Quartets*, we find the theme of fourness repeated twice, and in the first of these quartets, in the center of a circular pool, within a square garden, a vision occurs. It is an abandoned garden and the pool is empty— or so it seems.

Dry the pool, dry concrete, brown edged,
And the pool was filled with water out of sunlight,
And the lotos rose, quietly, quietly,
The surface glittered out of heart of light,
And they were behind us, reflected in the pool.
Then a cloud passed, and the pool was empty.[87]

In a moment of vision the drained pool becomes filled with luminous water, and the quiet center unfolds. Yet again, it is only a flash. There is a voice from the trees.

Go, go, go said the bird: human kind
Cannot bear very much reality.[88]

The Word reveals itself, and is gone. Yet the poet, through attention to language, is able to lead us toward the still point.

   Words, after speech, reach
Into the silence. Only by the form, the pattern,
Can words or music reach
The stillness, as a Chinese jar still
Moves perpetually in its stillness.
Not the stillness of the violin, while the note lasts
Not that only, but the co-existence,
Or say that the end precedes the beginning.[89]

It is only through pattern that words, music, and the Chinese jar reveal the still point. Thus Eliot weaves intricate patterns with words that are only secondary to the pure, silent design, the *maṇḍala*, they reveal. The *maṇḍala* is there before, during, and after the words. It is eternal. The words only reveal it. Just as the center of the *maṇḍala* is the summit of consciousness,

Eliot defines poetry as a people's "highest point of consciousness, its greatest power and most delicate sensibility."[90]

T. S. Eliot was a Christian and for him the still point was
Christ, the Divine Word. In order to touch this center, we must
travel through the patterns of words to the Word. It is a poetic,
linguistic process. It is also a process of prayer. In order to redeem
time we must redeem language, our instrument of revelation.
Rather than giving us the broken, fragmented language of *The
Waste Land*, Eliot, in his later poetry, becomes aware of the
incantatory, liturgical power of words. His poems are prayers, and
within these prayers are patterns and designs that appeal to the
deepest center of our being, that invoke the Word in mysterious
ways.

If the lost word is lost, if the spent word is spent
If the unheard, unspoken
Word is unspoken, unheard;
Still is the unspoken word, the Word unheard,
The Word without a word, the Word within
The world and for the world;
And the light shone in darkness and
Against the Word the unstilled world still whirled
About the centre of the silent Word.[91]

Eliot gives the unspoken, unheard Word, the Word without
a word, a voice. The "still" in the fourth line is important. It
means both "quiet" and "yet." Because the Word is so interior,
so *quiet*, it is unheard. *Yet* it quietly continues despite the inattention of the world.

To what can we attribute this inattention? Though prayer
and poetry can lead us toward the still point, we can never really
remain there. Why is it that Eliot prays,

Blessèd sister, holy mother, spirit of the fountain, spirit of the garden,
Suffer us not to mock ourselves with falsehood
Teach us to care and not to care
Teach us to sit still.[92]

Why is it that we cannot sit still? It is, perhaps, because we are inextricably bound up with language, with thoughts, with words, and words will not sit still; they

Crack and sometimes break, under the burden,
Under the tension, slip, slide, perish,
Decay with imprecision, will not stay in place,
Will not stay still.[93]

And this is precisely the problem in Western religious practice. We simply have not realized the linguisticality of our prayer. We have seen in the Vedic tradition that words *will* stand still. *Dhruva* is precisely the Word, firmly established in the highest Heaven, milking the essence of all being. The art of meditation through language is so highly developed in India that it is something of a science. Given the proper preparation, any of the experiences we find in the literature of the East are as repeatable as any scientific experiment. In the West, however, our attention has been focused on other matters. Consequently we have a more passive and negative orientation toward meditation. We find here no concise, precise linguistic formulas such as *mantras, koans,* and *sūtras.*

Furthermore, when we read the greatest Western exponents of prayers, we do not find prayer presented in terms that are attractive to many. We are told from the outset that we must renounce all things and proceed by a way of "darkness." Eliot, for instance, tells us that the way is one of

Internal darkness, deprivation
And destitution of all property,
Desiccation of the world of sense,
Evacuation of the world of fancy,
Inoperancy of the world of spirit.[94]

Or, in another passage,

Shall I say it again? In order to arrive there,
To arrive where you are, to get from where you are not,
    You must go by a way wherein there is no ecstasy.

In order to arrive at what you do not know
    You must go by a way which is the way of ignorance.
In order to possess what you do not possess
    You must go by the way of dispossession.
In order to arrive at what you are not
    You must go through the way in which you are not.
And what you do not know is the only thing you know
And what you own is what you do not own
And where you are is where you are not.[95]

This is austere language, language borrowed from the late-sixteenth-century Spanish mystic Saint John of the Cross, one of the most austere contemplatives in the Western tradition, who wrote,

To reach satisfaction in all
desire its possession in nothing.
To come to possess all
desire the possession of nothing.
To arrive at being all
desire to be nothing.
To come to the knowledge of all
desire the knowledge of nothing.
To come to the pleasure you have not
you must go by a way in which you enjoy not.
To come to the knowledge you have not
you must go by a way in which you know not.
To come to the possession you have not
you must go by a way in which you possess not.
To come to be what you are not
you must go by a way in which you are not.
When you turn toward something
you cease to cast yourself upon the all.
For to go from all to the all
you must deny yourself of all in all.
And when you come to the possession of the all
you must possess it without wanting anything.
Because if you desire to have something in all
your treasure in God is not purely your all.

In this nakedness the spirit finds
its quietude and rest.
For in coveting nothing,
nothing weighs it down,
because it is in the center of its humility.
When it covets something
in this very desire it is wearied.[96]

Although this may be appealing to some hermits, it is hardly the type of language to interest a lot of people in prayer. And that is not all. Saint John of the Cross, perhaps the West's greatest expert on prayer, informs us that we must abandon attachment to all things—friends, senses, and even spiritual phenomena such as visions—if we are even to begin the practice.

We would be very much in error if we supposed that this was due to any poverty of spirituality in the man. It simply resulted from the fact that he was a monk, and that he presented his knowledge of prayer in terms of the most severe asceticism. He was an immensely gifted contemplative. Not only was the depth of his experience of God unfathomable, and not only did he celebrate it in what is surely some of the world's most beautiful verse, but in his commentaries he left the definitive statement on prayer, at least in the Catholic tradition. Yet his poetry, with its echoing sonority and abysmally haunting imagery, remains unheard. The following poem is entitled "The Fountain" or "Song of the Soul That Rejoices in Knowing God Through Faith."

For well I know the spring that flows and runs
Though it is night.

That fountain, eternal, is well hidden,
And well I know where she springs,
Though it is night.

I do not know her origin, for she has none,
Yet I know that in her all things have their origin,
Though it is night.

I know there cannot be a thing of such beauty,
And that heavens and earth drink there,

Though it is night.

I know no one can fathom her depth,
And that no one can wade through her,
Though it is night.

Her clarity is never obscured,
And I know that all light comes from her,
Though it is night.

I know her streams so overflow,
They water infernos, heavens and all peoples,
Though it is night.

The stream that is born from this spring,
How well I know her power and force,
Though it is night.

This eternal spring is hidden
In this living bread to give us life,
Although it is night.

She calls to all creatures,
And in her waters they are satisfied, though it is dark,
Because it is night.

This living fountain for which I long,
In this bread of life I see.
Though it is night.[97]

The darkness of night is the most prominent image in the works of the saint. There is the darkness of leaving behind the joys of friendship, of the senses, and of the intellect. A second darkness is the darkness of faith, for it is only pure faith, relying on nothing else, that is a true guide. Another darkness is the darkness of renunciation of spiritual understandings and visions. Absorption in dark contemplation of the divine is so far beyond the realm of the senses, thoughts, feelings, imagination, understanding, or vision that all these must be renounced. There is an acute awareness that conceptions and thoughts *about* God are only *about*. They are not God.

How do you go on
O life, not living where you truly live?
And always dying
From the arrows which pierce you,
Your conceptions of the Beloved?[98]

There is, then, no guide, no method of approach except darkness over all that we have known before. The way calls for utter renunciation, faith, and ultimately love.

Dark Night

One dark night
Inflamed with love and longing.
O delightful flight!
Unseen, I slipped away,
All being still within my house.

In pitch blackness, secure,
I found a secret way.
O delightful flight!
In darkness,
All being still within my house.

In the joyous night
Secretly, unseen by anyone,
I saw nothing
And had no other light or guide
Save the fire, the fire inside.

This light guided me
More truly than the light of day,
To where one awaited me
Whom I knew well,
In a place where no one else appears.

O night my guide!
O night more lovely than the dawn!
O tender night that joined
Lover to Beloved
Transforming the lover in her loved one.

Upon my flowering breast,

Which I had saved for him alone,
He lay sleeping there.
And I caressed him
And a fan of cedars stirred the air.

The breeze from the ramparts,
When I was playing with his hair,
With its serene hand
Fell upon my neck, wounding it,
And suspending all my senses.

I lay abandoned, lost to myself,
And lay my face on my love.
All ceased. I left my being,
Leaving my cares
Forgotten among the lilies.[99]

It is no accident that Saint John of the Cross presented his teachings in terms of darkness and obscurity, for his own path in life was one of tremendous suffering. He was born Juan de Yepes y Álvarez in 1542 at Fontiveros, Spain, some twenty miles northwest of Ávila. His father, Gonzalo de Yepes, came from a wealthy family of silk merchants, but was disowned because he fell in love with, and married, a poor and humble weaver named Catalina Álvarez. Shortly after John's birth his father died, and the family then lived in extreme poverty. But John nevertheless succeeded in gaining an education under the Jesuits. At the age of twenty, he joined the Carmelites at the Monastery of Santa Ana in Medina del Campo. There he studied art and theology, and was soon ordained. It so happened that when John was singing his first mass in Medina del Campo he met Mother Teresa of Ávila, who was actively engaged in reforming monastic life so that there would be more time for prayer and contemplation. She met with John and employed his services, as he was eager to live a more prayerful life. At that time, however, the Church was reacting to the Protestant Reformation. The Protestants had come up with the notion that a Christian needs no middleman to reach God, and saw much of the authoritarianism and ritual of the Catholic

Church as meaningless and corrupt. They emphasized instead direct inner experience of God through prayer. The Catholic Church, to reassert its authority, emphasized ritual and became suspicious of anyone interested in prayer. Thus Mother Teresa's reform movement was suddenly suppressed and John ended up in a dungeon six feet wide and ten feet long, with no window. It was terribly cold in winter and suffocating in summer. Meals consisted of bread, water, and an occasional sardine. Three evenings each week the monks would take him from his cell and whip him. His wounds did not heal for years.

In the darkness of this prison, however, he experienced deep union with God and wrote poetry. Finally he escaped to southern Spain. Imprisonment and persecution, instead of making him cynical and bitter, had given him great compassion and enlightened him. The privations he had suffered, however, colored his attitude toward the interior life. The darkness of his prison cell is reflected in the imagery of his poetry and prose. It is unfortunate that the writings of this gentle, compassionate spiritual director should be so severe in tone, for they contain some of the most subtle knowledge of the psychology of prayer in the Christian tradition, and have imparted their tone to the many teachings that have drawn inspiration from them. For example, the Trappist monk Thomas Merton, who died in 1968, was deeply influenced by Saint John of the Cross and remains through his writings the greatest contemporary exponent of Christian contemplative prayer. We find in reading Merton that

the climate in which monastic prayer flowers is that of the desert, where the comfort of man is absent, where the secure routines of man's city offer no support, and where prayer must be sustained by God in the purity of faith. Even though he may live in a community, the monk is bound to explore the inner waste of his own being as a solitary. The Word of God which is his comfort is also his distress. The liturgy, which is his joy and which reveals to him the glory of God, cannot fill a heart that has not previously been humbled and emptied by dread. *Alleluia* is the song of the desert.[100]

Language such as this makes the richness of inner life unattractive to many and stands in stark contrast to the spiritual teachings of the East, where, although we find asceticism, we also find that some of the greatest saints have been married. Kabir, for instance, was a husband and weaver; one of the seers of the Upanishads had twelve wives; and the very incarnation of God, Krishna, dallied with thousands of milkmaids. Everyday life is compatible with spiritual awareness. In Zen, normal activity, complemented by a period of meditation, is the spiritual life.

The East has developed the art of meditation to such a degree that it has become something of a science. Rather than leaving the unfolding of the spiritual dimension to chance, the East has developed time-honored methods. While it is true that Western tradition has left us a rich legacy of spiritual teachings, we find in them neither awareness of the centrality of language to religion nor emphasis on specific techniques to overcome the bewitchment of words. It is little wonder that T. S. Eliot should plead, "Teach us to sit still," and that many Western contemplatives, following Merton's example, are looking to the linguistically subtle orientations of Zen and Hinduism to deepen that stillness. Both the yogis and the Zen masters realized long ago that both the demonic and the divine dwell in language—that language is the obstacle walling the seeker from divinity and the very form in which divinity is revealed.

Merton, being a Trappist monk deeply committed to prayer, was acutely aware of the Christian dependence upon symbols and language. A Christian contemplative is, after all, a part of the Church and must attempt to communicate his most intimate experiences in some theological form, using Christian language and symbols, so that they are theologically valid and understandable to his fellow Christians. He must make his experience communicable, and many mystics who have not bowed to canon have paid with their lives. Merton was impressed with Zen because of its absolute refusal to be easily communicable, and because it aims instead to blast away our comfortable symbolic network of communication in order to expose the stark nakedness of simple communion. Whereas Christian experience is valid only to the degree it approximates established symbols and theologically sanctioned forms, Zen attempts to do away with theology and symbols and to establish only the vital uniqueness of each living moment. The old dictum that "Zen teaches nothing" is true in the sense that it teaches no *thing*. And Merton, living in the era of Wittgenstein, was well aware of the bewitchment of language and Zen's capacity to overcome its spell as surely as the kiss of a princess transforms a frog into a prince. "The language used by Zen," Merton realized,

is therefore in some sense an antilanguage, and the "logic" of Zen is a radical reversal of philosophical logic. The human dilemma of communication is that we cannot communicate ordinarily without words and signs, but even ordinary experience tends to be falsified by our habits of verbalization and rationalization. The convenient tools of language enable us to decide beforehand what we think things mean, and tempt us all too easily to see things only in a way that fits our logical preconceptions and our verbal formulas. Instead of seeing *things* and *facts* as they are we see them as reflections and verifications of the sentences we have previously made up in our minds. We quickly forget how to simply *see* things and substitute our words and our formulas for the things themselves, manipulating facts so that we see only what conveniently fits our prejudices. Zen uses language against itself to blast out these preconceptions and to destroy the specious "reality" in our minds so that we can *see directly*. Zen is saying, as Wittgenstein said, "Don't think: Look!"[101]

The statements in the antilanguage of Zen are not really statements at all. They are, Merton realized, more like the ringing of an alarm clock. Some people are so deeply involved in their dreams that they do not even hear the alarm. Others hear it, turn it off, and then go back to sleep. The Buddha, walking through the forest after his enlightenment, was asked by a woodcutter if he was a God. He replied, "No, I am simply awake."

For all his admiration of what many of his fellow Christians would see as pagan and false traditions, Thomas Merton was a truly devout Christian. His personal example and writings have inspired and deepened the prayer life of thousands and allowed them to appreciate the religious experience of the whole of humankind. He was aware that in the First Epistle to the Corinthians, Saint Paul was careful to differentiate between the wisdom of words and the wisdom of the Word. True spirituality simply cannot dawn until this latter wisdom, which is beyond mere words, reveals itself.

Though Christianity has just recently realized the centrality of language to spirituality through writers such as Merton, it has a long tradition of language tending to concision—rather like the Eastern linguistic tools such as *mantras, sūtras,* and *koans* that owe part of their potency to their succinctness. Names are especially important in the Bible. Both the Jews and the Christians worship God "in his name." "In the beginning was the Word, and the Word was with God, and the Word was God," opens the Gospel of John. Since the presence of Jesus and his Father is a verbal presence, it is little surprise that among the early Christian monks of the first century A.D., in the deserts of Egypt and Syria, there existed only the barest rudiments of liturgy and philosophical discussion. The majority of their time was spend in prayer. This prayer consisted of invoking the name of Jesus Christ in the very deepest recess of the soul.

The desert fathers in the simplicity of their prayers had much in common with the seers of India, who had the divine Word as their central object of meditation. Such prayer, at its deepest levels, involves more listening than speaking. Can we truly say we listen, however, if we hear in this deep Word that transcends all words only the narrow theology of our local church? Let us, for a moment, turn to a man who devoted his life to the question of genuine listening in order that we may hear the full breadth of the Word.

One of India's greatest men, a renowned poet, philosopher, and linguist, was named Bhartrihari. He lived during the golden age of Indian culture, when philosophy, literature, and music flourished, crime was almost unheard of, and the internationally praised universities at Valabhi and Nālandā drew scholars from afar. It was in this setting that Bhartrihari found that if we speak truthfully and listen deeply, we share something of the experience of the seers. Even in normal conversation we participate to a greater or lesser degree in the very life of the Word.

We have all had the experience—when conversing with a friend or writing a letter, a paper, a poem, or a musical work—of intuitively glimpsing a vaguely felt idea, an abstract presence that seems to hover just beyond our mental grasp. This obscure something, which has not yet presented itself in the form of coherent thoughts or words, we experience as an intense desire for expression, a tumescent inevitability. The poet Diane Wakoski speaks of it as the "tumescent feeling the poet has, when he knows he has a poem bursting inside of him, and doesn't yet know its exact shape or its perfect process."[102] We wish to burst into speech or song, to say or sing in total resonance with what we feel. Yet after having attempted an expression, and even after numerous revisions, we are still haunted by that slippery something which somehow manages to elude us. It remains teasingly poised just beyond our reach, yet coiled with intense energy and ready to strike at any instant. Bhartrihari calls this something the *sphoṭa*, "that from which the meaning spurts or bursts forth." It is that something which Wakoski calls a "poem bursting inside." This *sphoṭa* is the meaning of a sentence or word and is eternally present in the mind of the speaker and the listener.

What happens during the process of speaking? The speaker must try to awaken in the listener the same eternal meaning, the same Word, that is seeking expression within himself. This Word is transformed by its own inner energy into the symbols and concepts and language of the speaker. The eternal, silent, undivided meaning of a sentence or word bursts into the mind of the speaker. The speaker's mind then grasps this Word and breaks it down into an audible sequence of sounds that exist in time. It is then the task of the listener to perceive these sounds and integrate them so that the same unitary and eternal *sphoṭa* or Word bursts forth in his own mind.

An analogy that may help us to appreciate Bhartrihari's

concept of the eternal meaning of a finite sentence bursting forth suddenly in the mind can be taken from mathematics. In fact, Wittgenstein uses this example to demonstrate how, in a flash, a finite series can reveal an infinite amount of information. When we see the finite series 1, 2, 3, 4 . . . we quite suddenly realize that it suggests an infinite set—all the counting numbers. Similarly, the finite series 1, 3, 5, 7 . . . suddenly suggests all the odd numbers. We ponder the series 3, 9, 27, 81 . . . and suddenly realize that it suggests the powers of 3. The realization of the infinite, eternal meaning behind the finite series appears instantaneously, in a flash. It is a lightninglike mental perception that reveals the *sphoṭa* or eternal meaning of a word or sentence and is awakened by the presence of a finite series of sounds. Since all sentences are, in essence, eternal, deep within even the most casual dialogue reside all the qualities and powers of deepest communion. If we listen deeply we can hear the Word.

In the introduction we said that to be human is to be engaged in conversation, in dialogue—whether our own ceaseless internal dialogue or conversation with friends. Yet dialogue breaks down and verbal abuse escalates into physical abuse. Within the simple syllables and words of which all our conflicting theories, philosophies, and systems of belief are built dwells the immense, infinite power of the Word. It is only among those who do not see the Word beyond words that there is argument and suffering. Harmony among humanity depends upon the depth of our listening, of our relationship with the Word.

Bhartrihari's insights into language and listening are especially viable in the intense encounter among cultures in today's world. To demonstrate the general applicability of Bhartrihari's findings, let us apply it to the experience of a hypothetical Christian hermit in Greece. We will call him Father Dionysios. He sits mornings on a cool straw mat within his simple hut at the foot of a mountain. It is just before dawn, and beyond the steep cliffs the sea spreads into darkness. Father Dionysios is praying alone, just as Jesus was often alone when he prayed. He prays as recluses on this mountain have done for centuries. He simply prays, *"Kyrie eleison"* (Jesus, have mercy). Were he to pronounce these words aloud they would have a slightly different timbre or intonation each time. He would certainly pronounce them with a different accent than some of his brother hermits from other regions of Greece. Bhartrihari would say that this is because sound, on this oral level, is subject to modification and distortion. Every time a word is pronounced, it comes out just a little bit differently. Bhartrihari would call this level Uttered Speech *(vaikhari)*.

Father Dionysios, then, does not audibly intone the prayer but simply worships silently in his mind. After some time, as the mist rises over the waters in the morning light, the faint sound of the prayer within Father Dionysios' mind undergoes a transformation. It seems as if he no longer thinks it himself, as if the voice of the prayer, the Word, wells up within his heart and makes itself heard and felt in a most sweet and silent manner. The sound of the prayer is here refined and purified of any individual characteristics of pronunciation. His absorption in meditation is so great that time seems to be overshadowed at moments by a sense of timelessness. Bhartrihari would call this deep mental absorption Middle Speech *(madhyamā),* because it lies midway between Uttered Speech and the utter silence of the deepest level of the Word.

Suddenly Father Dionysios may have a kind of vision in which the name of the Lord, the Word, becomes luminous and sonorous. Time and all other thoughts are dissolved. Because of its luminosity and the immediacy of the experience of the Word, Bhartrihari would call this Seeing Speech *(pashyanti).*

Finally the hermit, in the innermost essence of his prayer, may seem to enter into a most mysterious, boundless silence that is beyond all thoughts and words. Bhartrihari would call this Ultimate Speech, the Word in its highest value (Shabdha-brahman).

The spiritual fathers of the Greek Orthodox and Russian Orthodox traditions hold that such prayer to Jesus, simply intoning his name, contains within itself all the truths of the Bible in an abbreviated, condensed form—for it takes the mind to that silence which is not an absence but a fullness, a concentration of knowledge and love. Thus the Word is revealed by a word. The silence of God, the pure presence of the ineffable, is known.

As Saint John of the Cross wrote:

One word has been spoken by the Father:
This is His Son.
He speaks this Word forever in eternal silence,
And it should be heard in silence by the soul.

Ill. 44

The Stone,
the Star, and
the Oak

But though the Word is common, the many live
as though they had a wisdom of their own.

—HERACLITIUS

I can well imagine a religion in which there are
no doctrines, so that nothing is spoken.

—WITTGENSTEIN

Oaks abide. Yet no matter how firmly they are rooted, they are the type of tree most often struck by lightning. In this respect they stand on common ground with the deeply poetic, prayerful attitude that is so vulnerable to bolts of sudden illumination. In European antiquity the oak was the most sacred of all things. In it the voices of the Gods were heard, and it was praised by the ancient bards as the granter of visions. These bards were something between poets, seers, and priests.

Visions, however, flee as suddenly as lightning sucked back up into the black belly of a cloud. And when the visions vanished, only the oak and the priestly functions of the former seers endured, leaving a petrified institution in the shadow of a departed era of intuition. The oak itself rather than the vision it revealed became the holy of holies. To break a twig from a sacred bough was a sin; and should a hapless commoner peel the bark from the trunk of the holy tree the culprit would pay with his life, his navel cut out with a knife and nailed to the wounded part of the oak. The integrity of the priestly symbol becomes more important than the integrity of the living human form.

Unlike oaks, our thoughts and feelings constantly shift. In their birth, fleeting life, and death we sense our own impermanence. Thoughts will not stand still like stones, mountains, or mosques. They will not abide like a God upon its lotus throne, the immutable words within a holy book, or a prince and princess in a fairy tale, living happily ever after.

William Blake, seer that he was, proclaimed that the visionary fire of intuition and imagination is continuously forging new poetic forms within the creative eye of the mind. The instant that vision is institutionalized, however, the eye blinks shut. The vision loses its luminous life in the vibrant domain of poetry and becomes transformed into stone, the petrified possession of the priest. It was the priest, not the poet, who sliced open the human breast and offered the blood at the foot of the oak. For Blake these Druidic rites were proof of what happens when we die poetically and become the victims of our own symbols.

Prayers also abide. And prayers are cows. But understanding this requires the imagination of a nomad four thousand years ago in India. Waking in the black silence before dawn to the immemorial chore of milking, day after day, year after year, it has always been the same—the warm milk steaming in the chill air as it hisses into the leather bags. Prayers are cows. They can be milked only when they stand firmly, steadily, contentedly. If the cow or prayer is restless it is not easy to milk and the milk is not good anyway. The seers of this tribe of nomads know this and their chore is another kind of milking. In the dark silence of their hearts they somehow *see* poetic prayers, sacred words swelling like udders and streaming luminous meaning until the heart, deeply absorbed, settles on an inmost brightness.

"To think truly," said Heidegger, "is to confine oneself to a single thought which one day stands still like a star in the world's sky." The chore of the seer, four thousand years ago in India, was just that—to milk the brightness of the Word as it abided, like

Ill. 45

a cow, in the sky of the mind, flooding the mind with a thousand streams of vision. Thus four thousand years later cows remain holy. And we can only begin to understand how holy they are when we learn that in the *Ananga Ranga*, an ancient Indian encyclopedia of sexual poses, of the myriad postures only one is said to confer great spiritual merit. It is called the Cow Posture. The woman positions herself on hands and feet (*not* knees and elbows) and the man "enjoys her like a bull." The details of this heaven-conferring act are left to the fertile imagination of what remains, even today, a predominantly rural population. And so it is that today India is an entire subcontinent of holy cows hanging like some giant udder from the belly of malnourished Asia.

Directly above this sacred subcontinent, it is said, and as

steady as a holy cow, stands the Pole Star. Just below rises Meru, the celestial mountain of the Gods. Flowing down its slopes is the sacred Goddess and river Ganges, dotted with hermitages and temples, and having waters sweet as blossoms. Blue lotuses are her eyes and red lotuses her mouth. The playful frontal mounds of bathing elephants are her breasts, her thighs are broad islands of dark sand, and her navel is a deep whirlpool. The entire universe, we learn, whirls about a central axis extending from the Pole Star down into the sacred subcontinent like a holy fig tree, situating India securely at the navel of creation.

If we could travel to Renaissance Italy, the city of Florence to be exact, and ask any person on the street the form of the cosmos, we would find that his view conformed, in its basic design, to the Indian model. We would find here also the blessings of a Goddess of sorts, flowing down upon the inhabitants of this little community on the Arno River, though we would hardly find her described in the Indian mode.

The universe, according to the Renaissance gentleman, is perfectly geometric. The Earth is a sphere in the center, nested within a series of concentric spheres. All these turn about a central axis. Presiding over all, of course, above the topmost sphere, God the Father abides on his holy throne, as steady as the Pole Star.[103] If we were to express any doubt that this was the basic pattern of things, our informant would be quick to take out a map of Florence, a bird's-eye view, to demonstrate that the city itself is modeled after the universal pattern, the sphere of the Earth resounding in a sort of Pythagorean harmony with the tune of the Creator.

In the very center of the map, and greatly exaggerated in size, looms the dome of a civic building. Around this commanding hub the streets of the city are laid out in a series of concentric rings. Outside the city wall, to the right, is the Pratello della Giustizia, the "Little Meadow of Justice," where criminals were hanged in public. The civic building and surrounding city repeat the pattern of the Renaissance cosmos, as does the typical Renaissance painting of the Last Judgment.

VEDUTA PROSPETTICA DI FIRENZE (1470 CIRCA)

FIORENZA

Ill. 46

Christ, like the central dome, appears in such paintings of that fateful day as a central, elevated, and enlarged figure. He sits towering above all, like a judge on a throne. Just below him, in the center of the composition, are his Apostles. The Virgin Mother is to his right. At his feet an angel with a trumpet summons all the souls. Also to his right are all those good souls who have been judged and will go to Paradise. On his left, in the same position as the Little Meadow of Justice (as viewed by Jesus if he *were* the central civic dome), stand all those who will be condemned to eternal fire.

Florentine artists such as Botticelli were called upon to cover the walls of civic institutions not with paintings of Venus, but with images of the Holy Virgin and the Last Judgment, so that the populace of this little community on the Arno would have no doubt that secular authority and divine blessings flowed straight from above. Every work of art, whether painting, sculpture, or architecture, thus reinforced the message. In the Holy Roman Empire it was not unusual to see paintings of the Last Judgment hanging prominently on the wall behind the judge's bench in a court of law. Spiritual symbolism served the purposes of political authority and propaganda.

Now late in the evening of July 20, 1501, one Antonio di Giuseppe Rinaldeschi, a young man belonging to a noble Florentine family, was making his way home from an evening of cards. He had been drinking, it seems, and was angry at having lost when he came upon a little church displaying above the door a painting of the Annunciation. In his frustration and intoxication, he picked up a piece of horse dung and hurled it deftly at the image, scoring a direct hit. Had the image been a statue of the Buddha and young Antonio a young Zen monk, the incident might well have gone down in Zen history as an act of Zen piety. Unfortunately for Antonio, however, the Catholic authorities had not acquired the Zen tradition of poking fun at themselves. The blasphemy did not escape the attention of a child, who reported the incident. Antonio's fate is well known in Florentine history. The next day he was arrested, summoned before the court, and tried at midnight of the same day. Then at precisely seven o'clock in the evening of holy Saint Mary Magdalene's Day (July 22) in 1501, Antonio di Giuseppe Rinaldeschi, the blasphemer, was hanged in public. The last thing he saw in his mortal body was a painting held against his face by a devout monk so that the victim could kiss the image of the holy Crucifixion with his last breath.

The citizens of Florence slept soundly that night, secure in the knowledge that their symbol system, the sacred axis of their universe, was unbroken; that the Holy Virgin had been appeased; and that her blessings would continue to flow down upon the city.

Like the citizens of Renaissance Florence, the members of archaic tribal societies carefully attempt to preserve their central symbols. The Arunta, an aboriginal tribe of central Australia, once led a life of wandering. In the ancient days, their elders told them, a sacred post stood at the very hub of the world. The Creator, Numbakula, carved this pole from the gum tree known as the eucalyptus and then scaled it, disappearing forever into the sky world. And this is why the clan, long ago, began to carry a eucalyptus pole on their shoulders as they wandered about in the direction it seemed to point. Once, a team of ethnologists informs us, the pole broke. The clan wandered about lost for some time and finally lay down to die. Their axis was broken and communication with the world above was no longer possible. Life was simply not worth living. If you do not kill your Buddha, he may kill you. In India, the word for suffering is *duḥkha*. It means, literally, "having a bad axle." The axis, while providing a society with a sense of center, can also act as a prison and even a tomb. Renaissance Florence, as the map illustrates, was enclosed by a lock and chain.

Any symbol system that does not encourage transcendence becomes a prison. "The art of free society," said Alfred North Whitehead, "consists first in the maintenance of the symbolic code; and secondly in the fearlessness of revision, to secure that the code serves those purposes which satisfy an enlightened reason. Those societies which cannot combine reverence to their symbols with freedom of revision, must ultimately decay either from anarchy, or from the slow atrophy of a life stifled by useless shadows."[104]

Through reverence a re-vision comes about naturally. In deepest worship the symbol becomes a visionary presence and is revised, if need be, by the silent luminosity in which it basks. Such a re-vision would have allowed the Arunta to see that stillness which is the true center of all moving things, and to cut, perhaps, another pole. But when all was said and done the symbol prevailed, the tree becoming more important than the tribe.

So it is with the symbol-using animal. We so easily become the pawns and prisoners of öur own symbols, bearing them like crosses or eucalypti. We play our language-games but somehow lose the sense of play. Yet in the East we find a certain wisdom of reverence. For the Hindus, Taoists, and Buddhists, in their awareness of the enchantress Language, never forget that element of play in worship. For them the world is the amorous embrace of the Goddess Speech; it is the music of Krishna's flute, structur-

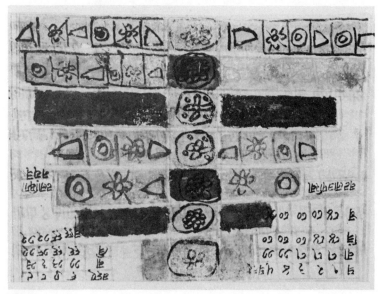

Ill. 47

ing a million galaxies; it is *lilā*, "divine play." And the Zen master who thunders, "Shut up!" when asked the meaning of Zen by a particularly pensive student displays this same sense of play. He is not only suggesting that language and life are essentially sportive, but demonstrating the futility of loquacity in such ponderous matters and pointing instead to the eloquence of that silence transcending even the oak, the star, and the stone.

Notes

1. Arthur J. Arberry, trans., *The Koran Interpreted*, 2 vols. (New York: Macmillan, 1973), 2:50–61.
2. Translated by the author from the Koran, 2:96.
3. Robinson Jeffers, "Roan Stallion," *Roan Stallion, Tamar, and Other Poems* (New York: Horace Liveright, 1925), p. 24.
4. Annie Dillard, "Teaching a Stone to Talk," *Atlantic*, February 1981.
5. Harold Stewart, trans., *A Chime of Windbells* (Rutland, Vermont: Charles E. Tuttle Co., 1970), p. 57.
6. Albert Einstein, *The World as I See It* (New York: Covici-Friede, 1934), p. 138.
7. Hugh Kenner, *The Pound Era* (Los Angeles: University of California Press, 1971), p. 123.
8. Ibid., p. 97.
9. Robert Bly, *The Kabir Book: Forty-four of the Ecstatic Poems of Kabir* (Boston: Beacon Press, 1977), p. 35.
10. On Vedic poetics see Jan Gonda, *Vedic Literature* (Wiesbaden: Otto Harrassowitz, 1975).
11. Ludwig Wittgenstein, *Zettel*, trans. G. E. M. Anscombe and

ed. G. E. M. Anscombe and G. H. von Wright (Oxford: Basil Blackwell, 1967), par. 160.

12.   See, for instance, Rigveda 1.25.16, 1.114.9, 10.127.8, 1.173.3, 9.94.2, 3.57.1, 10.71.3, 4.41.5, 8.100.11, 2.2.9.

13.   Raimundo Panikkar, *The Vedic Experience, Mantramañjari* (Los Angeles: University of California Press, 1971), p. 101.

14.   Robert Bly, *The Kabir Book,* p. 52.

15.   Ibid., p. 21.

16.   Hare Hongi, "A Maori Cosmogony," *Journal of the Polynesian Society* 16 (1907), pp. 113–14.

17.   Ibid., p. 114.

18.   Rigveda 1.164.41–42, translated by the author.

19.   Chāndogya Upanishad 1.1, translated by the author.

20.   Czeslaw Milosz, "Notes," *Bells in Winter* (New York: Ecco Press, 1978), p. 34.

21.   Jonathan Shear, "Maharishi, Plato and the TM-Sidhi Program on Innate Structures of Consciousness," *Metaphilosophy* 12:1 (1981), p. 73. See also Shear's "Plato, Piaget, and Maharishi on Cognitive Development," read to the American Psychological Association's Eighty-sixth Annual Convention, Toronto, August 1978, and reprinted in *Scientific Research on the Transcendental Meditation Program: Collected Papers,* Vol. II (MERU Press, forthcoming).

22.   Jonathan Shear, "Maharishi, Plato," p. 74.

23.   Rigveda 1.164.10.

24.   Czeslaw Milosz, "Tidings," *Bells in Winter,* p. 5.

25.   Hugh Kenner, *The Pound Era,* p. 171.

26.   Mircea Eliade, *Birth and Rebirth* (New York: Harper and Brothers, 1958), p. 95.

27.   From John Brzostoski's introduction to *Tantra: From the Collection of Blance Manso* (Santa Barbara, Calif.: Santa Barbara Museum of Art, 1970), pp. 9–10.

28.   John G. Neihardt, *Black Elk Speaks: Being the Life Story of a Holy Man of the Oglala Sioux* (New York: William Morrow and Co., 1932), p. 43.

29.   This and the above quote are from Swami Nikhilananda, trans., *The Gospel of Sri Ramakrishna* (New York: Ramakrishna-Vivekananda Center, 1942), pp. 396, 778–79.

30.   The entire case history of the woman is contained in Gerhard

Adler, *Living Symbol,* Bollingen Series LXIII (New York: Pantheon Books, 1961).

31.   Wallace Stevens, "A Primitive Like an Orb," *The Palm at the End of the Mind: Selected Poems and a Play,* ed. Holly Stevens (New York: Vintage Books, 1972), pp. 317–20.

32.   William Meredith, "Ideogram," *The Cheer* (New York: Alfred A. Knopf, 1980), p. 35.

33.   Richard Wilhelm's translation rendered into English by Cary F. Baynes, *The I Ching or Book of Changes,* Bollingen Series XIX (Princeton, N.J.: Princeton University Press, 1967), p. 201.

34.   Burton Watson, trans., and William Theodore de Bary, ed., *The Complete Works of Chuang Tzu, Records of Civilization: Sources and Studies,* No. LXXX (New York: Columbia University Press, 1968), pp. 187–88.

35.   Ibid., pp. 63–65.

36.   Ibid., p. 67.

37.   Ibid., p. 35.

38.   Ibid., pp. 240–41.

39.   Ibid., pp. 42–44.

40.   Gary Zukav, *The Dancing Wu Li Masters: An Overview of the New Physics* (New York: William Morrow and Co., 1979), p. 117.

41.   Burton Watson, trans., *The Complete Works of Chuang Tzu,* pp. 234–35.

42.   Herbert L. Samuel, *Essay in Physics* (New York: Harcourt, Brace and Co., 1952), pp. 50ff.

43.   This rendering is by the author.

44.   Ludwig Wittgenstein, "Lecture on Ethics," *Philosophical Review,* 74:1 (1965), pp. 13–16.

45.   Ibid., pp. 11–12.

46.   Ludwig Wittgenstein, *Philosophical Investigations,* trans. C. E. M. Anscombe (Oxford: Basil Blackwell, 1953), par. 111.

47.   Philip Kapleau, *The Three Pillars of Zen* (Boston: Beacon Press, 1967), p. 135.

48.   Katsuki Sekida, *Zen Training: Methods and Philosophy* (New York, Tokyo: Weatherhill, 1975), p. 99.

49.   Sohaku Ogata, trans., *Zen for the West* (London: Rider and Co., 1959), pp. 98–99.

50.   Sodô, translated by the author.

51.   Cor van den Heuvel, ed., *The Haiku Anthology: English Language Haiku by Contemporary American and Canadian Poets* (Garden City, N.Y.: Anchor Books, 1974), p. 163.
52.   Issa, translated by the author.
53.   This and preceding poems by Busson and Basho have been translated by the author.
54.   Ryôta, translated by the author.
55.   Paul Reps, ed., *Zen Flesh, Zen Bones: A Collection of Zen and Pre-Zen Writings* (Garden City, N.Y.: Anchor Books), pp. 136–54.
56.   For a delightful view of the New Physics see Edwin A. Abbott, *Flatland: A Romance of Many Dimensions,* ed. Banesh Hoffman (New York: Dover Publications, 1952).
57.   William Blake, *Jerusalem,* 15:8–9.
58.   Ibid., 55:43–46.
59.   William Blake, *Milton,* 28:44–59.
60.   William Blake, *The First Book of Urizen,* 3:8–10.
61.   William Blake, *Milton,* 32:16–23.
62.   Robert F. Gleckner, "Most Holy Forms of Thought: Some Observations on Blake and Language," *English Literary History,* No. 41 (1974), pp. 555–77.
63.   William Blake, *Jerusalem,* 88:3–5.
64.   Ibid., 98:24–43.
65.   Ibid., 86:1–10.
66.   Ibid., 29–30.
67.   William Blake, "Mock on, Mock on Voltaire, Rousseau," 11:9–12.
68.   William Blake, *The Marriage of Heaven and Hell,* 11.
69.   William Blake, *Milton,* 28:62–29:3.
70.   William Blake, *The First Book of Urizen,* 3:18–20.
71.   William Blake, *Jerusalem,* 5:17–20.
72.   William Blake, "Description of a Vision of the Last Judgment."
73.   Mundaka Upanishad, 2.2.4.
74.   William Blake, letter to Thomas Butts, November 22, 1802.
75.   William Blake, letter to Thomas Butts, October 2, 1800, 45–62.
76.   William Blake, "The Tyger," 1–4, *Songs of Experience.*
77.   Frank Waters, *Book of the Hopi* (New York: Ballantine

Books, 1971), p. 7.

78.   Benjamin Lee Whorf, *Language, Thought and Reality,* ed.
John B. Carroll (Boston: Massachusetts Institute of Technology,
1956), p. 150.

79.   Frank Waters, *Book of the Hopi,* pp. 2–28

80.   After George Bird Brinnell, *Blackfoot Lodge Tales* (New
York: Charles Scribner's Sons, 1892), pp. 104–7.

81.   Ezek. 37:1–8, quoted in Mircea Eliade, *Shamanism: Archaic
Techniques of Ecstasy,* Bollingen Series LXXVI, trans. Willard
R. Trask (Princeton, N.J.: Princeton University Press, 1972),
pp. 162–63.

82.   T. S. Eliot, "Ash Wednesday," *The Complete Poems and
Plays, 1909–1950* (New York: Harcourt, Brace and World,
1971), p. 61.

83.   C. G. Jung, *Concerning Mandala Symbolism, The Collected
Works of C. G. Jung,* Vol. 9, Bollingen Series XX (Princeton,
N.J.: Princeton University Press, 1969–79), p. 357.

84.   T. S. Eliot, "East Coker," *Four Quartets, Complete Poems,* p.
129.

85.   T. S. Eliot, "The Dry Salvages," *Four Quartets, Complete
Poems,* p. 136.

86.   T. S. Eliot, "Burnt Norton," *Four Quartets, Complete Poems,*
p. 119.

87.   Ibid., p. 118.

88.   Ibid.

89.   Ibid., p. 121.

90.   T. S. Eliot, *The Use of Poetry and the Use of Criticism*
(Totowa, N.S.: Barnes and Noble, 1975), p. 5.

91.   T. S. Eliot, "Ash Wednesday," p. 65.

92.   Ibid., p. 67.

93.   T. S. Eliot, "Burnt Norton," p. 121.

94.   Ibid., pp. 120–21

95.   T. S. Eliot, "East Coker," p. 127.

96.   Kieran Kavanaugh and Otilio Rodriguez, trans., *The Collected
Works of St. John of the Cross* (Washington, D.C.: Institute of
Carmelite Studies Publications, 1964), pp. 103–4.

97.   Translation by the author.

98.   Translation by the author.

99.   Translation by the author.

100.   Thomas Merton, *Contemplative Prayer* (Garden City, N.Y.: Image Books, 1971), p. 27.
101.   Thomas Merton, *Zen and the Birds of Appetite* (New York: New Directions, 1968), pp. 48–49.
102.   Diane Wakoski, "Variations on a Theme (An Essay on Revision)," *Sparrow*, No. 50 (November 1976).
103.   On the concept of cosmos in Florentine art, and the story of Antonio Giuseppe Rinaldeschi which follows, see Samuel Y. Edgerton, Jr., "Icons of Justice," *Past and Present*, 1980, No. 89, pp. 23-38.
104.   Alfred North Whitehead, *Symbolism: Its Meaning and Effect* (New York: Macmillan, 1927), p. 88.

Illustrations

1. "The Tree of Ages." Rajasthan, eighteenth century; Ajit Mookerjee Collection, New Delhi. (Reprinted by permission of Thames and Hudson, from Phillip Rawson, *Tantra*, p. 113)
2. Stonehenge. (Courtesy of the British Tourist Authority, 680 Fifth Avenue, New York, N.Y. 10019)
3. The Unicorn. (Lascaux)
4. The Sorceror of Les Trois Frères.
5. The Indo-European family of languages.
6. "Krishna with a Flute: Gopas and cows, water with expanded rose, lotuses." Indian, Rajput Pahari, Jamu, seventeenth century, .241 × .162 17.2804, Ross Coomaraswamy Collection. (Courtesy, Museum of Fine Arts, Boston)
7. A stylized form of the syllable "Om," with all the Gods contained within it. Rajasthan, eighteenth century. (Reprinted by permission of Thames and Hudson, from Phillip Rawson, *Tantra*, p. 127)
8. "Vāk-devī," the Goddess of Speech. The Goddess represents the subtle Word by which the universe comes into existence. In her reside all the Gods. Rajasthan, seventeenth century. (Reprinted by

247

permission of Thames and Hudson, from Ajit Mookerjee and Madhu Khanna, *The Tantric Way*, p. 8)

9. The spiritual region of enlightenment beyond the crown of the head, including the Pole Star, the Sun, the Moon, and the Cosmic Axis in the form of a flagpole atop the Cosmic Mountain. The domes of the Indian buildings conform to the structure of this region. Rajasthan, eighteenth century; Ajit Mookerjee Collection, New Delhi. (Reprinted by permission of Thames and Hudson, from Phillip Rawson, *Tantra*, p. 119)

10. The Shri Yantra

11. Sketches of experiences gained through meditation on the Pole Star sūtra. (Courtesy of Jonathan Shear, from "Maharishi, Plato and the TM-Sidhi Program on Innate Structures of Consciousness," *Metaphilosophy* 12:1 January 1981)

12. The structure of the cosmos as described in the myth of Er in Plato's *Republic*. (Courtesy of Jonathan Shear, from "Maharishi, Plato and the TM-Sidhi Program on Innate Structures of Consciousness," Metaphilosophy 12:1 January 1981)

13. "Pennant and Birds." Indian Tantric painting, eighteenth century. (Courtesy of Blanche Manso)

14. The tree of vibratory centers in the human body. The transcendent lotus or crown *chakra* opens above the top of the head. Rajasthan, eighteenth century. (Reprinted by permission of Thames and Hudson, from Phillip Rawson, *Tantra*, p. 85)

15. A design from a shaman's drum, showing the Cosmic Tree ascending to the sky world. The circle at top is the smokehole and the Pole Star. (Redrawn by Rosanna W. Lenorak from R. Cook, *The Tree of Life*)

16. A Tantric painting from India, eighteenth century. (Courtesy of Blanche Manso, from *Tantra: From the Collection of Blanche Manso*)

17. The vibratory centers in the human body. (Reprinted by permission of Thames and Hudson, from Ajit Mookerjee and Madhu Khanna, *The Tantric Way*, p. 15)

18. The Shri Yantra

19. The ground plan and elevation of the Barabadur Stupa, based on the Shri Yantra. (Reprinted by permission of Peter Bridgewater, from Madhu Khanna, *Yantra*, p. 148)

20. Head of Buddha. (Rosanna W. Lenorak)

21. "Black Elk at the Center of the Earth." (Reprinted by permission of the John G. Niehardt Trust, from John G. Niehardt, *Black Elk Speaks*, published by Simon & Schuster and the University of Nebraska Press)

22. "Seven Virgins Being Transformed." (*Songe de Poliphile*, 117, p. 61)

23. "The Metal Ring." (Reprinted by permission of Princeton University Press, from Gerhard Adler, *The Living Symbol: A Case Study in the Process of Individuation*, p. 104)

24. "Jewel Between Man and Woman." (Reprinted by permission of Princeton University Press, from Gerhard Adler, *The Living Symbol: A Case Study in the Process of Individuation*, p. 105)

25. "The Fight with the Angel." (Reprinted by permission of Princeton University Press, from Gerhard Adler, *The Living Symbol: A Case Study in the Process of Individuation*, plate 15)

26. "The Night Sky Mandala." (Reprinted by permission of Princeton University Press, from Gerhard Adler, *The Living Symbol: A Case Study in the Process of Individuation*, plate 16)

27. "Winged Youth." (Reprinted by permission of Princeton University Press, from Gerhard Adler, *The Living Symbol: A Case Study in the Process of Individuation*, plate 30)

28. "Clearing Autumn Skies Over Mountains and Valleys." Attributed to Kuo Hsi, Sung dynasty, twelfth century. (Courtesy of the Freer Gallery of Art, Smithsonian Institution, Washington, D.C.)

29. The circular arrangement of the sixty-four hexagrams of the I Ching.

30. The vibratory centers in the human body as understood in China.

31. "Realms of the Immortals." Sung dynasty, thirteenth century. (Courtesy of the Freer Gallery of Art, Smithsonian Institution, Washington, D.C.)

32. "Hsiang-yen and the Bamboos." Kano Motonobu. (Reprinted by permission of the Tokyo National Museum)

33. "A Solitary Angler." Attributed to Mo Yuan. (Reprinted by permission of the Tokyo National Museum)

34. From "Ten Bulls." Kakuan; transcribed by Nyogen Senzaki and Paul Reps; illustrated by Tomikichiro Tokuriki. From *Zen Flesh, Zen Bones: A Collection of Zen and Pre-Zen Writings*. (Reprinted by permission of Paul Reps)

35.   "An Early Zen Patriarch Tearing Up a Scroll of Scriptures." Attributed to Liang K'ai. (Courtesy of Takanaru Mitsui)

36.   "Ten Bulls." Kakuan; transcribed by Nyogen Senzaki and Paul Reps; illustrated by Tomikichiro Tokuriki. From *Zen Flesh, Zen Bones: A Collection of Zen and Pre-Zen Writings.* (Reprinted by permission of Paul Reps) Another version of the "Ten Bulls" shows, in the penultimate painting, the moon and the Little Dipper constellation turning about the Pole Star which is the star at the tip of the handle.

37.   "The Tyger." William Blake. (Courtesy of the Library of Congress)

38.   "Newton." William Blake. (Reprinted by permission of The Tate Gallery, London)

39.   A doughnut intersecting a plane. (Reprinted by permission of Wildwood House, London, and by special arrangement with Shambala Publications, Inc., 1920 13th Street, Boulder, Colorado 80302. From *The Tao of Physics,* © 1975 by Fritjof Capra.)

40.   "The World Egg." Rajasthan, eighteenth century. (Reprinted by permission of Thames and Hudson, from Ajit Mookerjee and Madhu Khanna, *The Tantric Way,* p. 91)

41.   "Durgā." Indian, eighteenth century. (Courtesy of Blanche Manso, from *Tantra: From the Collection of Blanche Manso*)

42.   Hopi symbols of the human body, the *kiva,* and the Earth. (Courtesy of Viking Penguin, Inc., from Frank Waters, *Book of the Hopi,* p. 29)

43.   "École de Durer: Le Christ en Croix." (Reprinted by permission of the Musée des Beaux-Arts de Rennes)

44.   "Square, Triangle, and Circle." Sengai. (Reprinted by permission of the Idemitsu Museum of Arts, Tokyo)

45.   All the gods residing in the syllable "Om." Rajasthan, eighteenth century. (Reprinted by permission of Thames and Hudson, from Phillip Rawson, *Tantra,* p. 38)

46.   "Map With a Chain." ca. 1485. (Reprinted by permission of the Istituto Geografico Militare, Florence)

47.   Levels of the radiant Cosmic Tree, in which the levels of the Universe are seen. Rajasthan, eighteenth century; Ajit Mookerjee Collection, New Delhi. (Reprinted by permission of Thames and Hudson, from Phillip Rawson, *Tantra,* p. 113)

Index

Aborigines, Australian, 79
Achilles, 157–158, 172
Adler, Gerhard, 91
Akshara, 53, 60, 67. *See also* Language of
   Eternity; Language of Syllables.
Allah, 14
Ananga Ranga, 234
Ant People, 195ff.
Apocalypse, 167, 174, 175
Apollo, 160
Apostles, 237
Archetype, 43, 73
Aristotle, 172
Arunta, 238, 239
Aryan tribes, 68
"Ash Wednesday" (Eliot), 43
Axis of the World, 68
Axle Tree, 76

Balts, 68
Basho, 140
Bégouën, Count Henri, 30
Bells in Winter (Milosz), 89

Bhartrihari, 225–229
Bible, the, 135, 225, 228
Black Elk, 88
Blackfoot Indians, 208ff.
Black Hills, 88
Black Stone, 14
Black Waters, 120
Blake, William, 158, 163–177, 233
Book of Changes, The (I Ching), 106, 108
Bo Tree, 139
Botticelli Sandro, 237
Bow Clan, 200
Brihadāranyaka Upanishad. *See* Great For-
   est Teaching.
Buber, Martin, 21
Buccho, 140
Buddha, 33, 79, 87, 105, 135–136, 138,
   140, 141, 174
Buddha-nature, 142
Buddhism, 128–139
Buddhist philosophy, 182
Buddhists, 211, 239
Buffalo, 208–211

Busson, 141
Butterfly Maidens, 180, 181

Carmelites, 221
Carpenter Shih, 116–117
Catholic Church, 222
Celestial Kingdom, 102, 124
Celtic Druids, 68
Center of the World, 87ff., 95
Chakra, 80, 84, 87
Ch'i, 116
China, 105, 142
Chinese ideograms, 42, 103–104
Chinese language, 37
Christ, 174, 215, 225, 237
Christianity, 211, 225
Christians, 211
Ch'u, 116
Chuang Tzu, 115ff., 117ff., 128, 130
Confucianists, 123–124
Conqueror of Indra, 49–50
Corn Mother, 190, 191
Cosmic Axis, 79, 87, 109, 110, 181
Cosmic Pillar, 68, 75
Cosmic Tree, 79, 80, 84, 85, 95, 99, 110, 138, 168, 174
Cow Posture, 234
Cows, 53
Creation Song, 187, 188, 189
Creator, 50, 180, 181, 190, 192, 193, 194, 204
Crooked Shaft, 116
crown *chakra*, 169

DA, 42, 49, 53, 55, 213
Dancing Wu Li Masters, The (Zukav), 120
"Dark Night" (Saint John of the Cross), 220
Dāru, 68
Democritus, 37, 159, 161, 170
Demon, 16
Descartes, René, 44, 160
Dhārana, 69, 183
Dharma, 75, 123, 135–136
Dhruva, 68, 69, 75, 183, 216
Dhyāna, 70
Dialogue, 16
Dickinson, Emily, 84
Dillard, Annie, 32, 89, 160
Dionysios, Father, 227–229
Donares eih, 68

Do-Nothing-Say-Nothing, 121
Dorw, 67, 68, 69
Dreams, 15
Druidic rites, 233
Druids, 67, 68, 69
Dubiety Dismissed, 121
Duncan, Robert, 42
Durgā, 176

Earth, 53, 62, 63, 104, 107, 110, 114, 185
Echo, 187
Einstein, Albert, 39, 159, 160, 162–163, 164, 167
Eliot, T. S., 41, 42, 43, 211ff., 223
English language, 22, 37, 52, 181
Er, myth of, 76, 78
Eskimos, 43
Essay in Physics (Samuel), 122
Eternal, the, 171
Eternity, 169, 171, 175
Ethics, 130
Europe, 41, 213
Events, 182
Ezekiel, 211, 212

Father, 181
Father Sun, 181, 192
Fire Clan, 196
First People, 181, 189, 192, 194
Flatland, 156–157, 158, 163
Flood, the, 174
Florence, 235
"Fountain, The" (Saint John of the Cross), 218
Four Quartets (Eliot), 214
Four Symbols, 106
France, 30
Freud, Sigmund, 43

Gabriel, Angel, 14
Galapagos Islands, 24ff.
Gamow, George, 23
Ganges Plain, 49
Ganges River, 235
Ginsberg, Allen, 42
Giuseppe Rinaldeschi, Antonio di, 237–238
God, 14, 15, 16, 21, 22, 24, 48, 60, 130, 158, 219, 222, 229
Goddess of Fire, 176
Goddess of the Word, 62 63

Goddess Speech, 239
God of Thunder, Baltic, 68
Gods, 41, 56, 105, 171, 174, 232, 235
Golden Egg, 174, 175
Gorillas, 33–34
Great Extreme, 106
Great Forest Teaching, (Brihadāranyaka Upanishad), 41, 48, 53, 55
Great Hunt, 30
Greece, 76, 78, 227
Greek language, 39
Greek Orthodox tradition, 228
Greeks, 37, 68
Guerrillas, 14, 15
Gum Tree, Australian, 79
Gutei, 133

Haiku, 42, 139–142
Harney Peak, 88
Heaven, 14, 53, 62, 63, 68, 75, 76, 104, 107, 110, 114, 117
Hegel, Georg Wilhelm Friedrich, 44
Heidegger, Martin, 233
Hell, 138
Heraclitus, 98, 99
Hexagrams, Sixty-four, 107
Hindu Kush, 68
Hindus, 239
Hira, Mount, 13–14
Hiranyagharba, 174
Holy Roman Empire, 237
Holy Virgin, 237
Hopi Indians, 37, 180–205
Hopi language, 181–185
Hui Tzu, 117

Ice Age, 30, 49
I Ching. See Book of Changes.
Ideal Forms, 78
Ideogram, Chinese, 103ff.
India, 39, 41, 55, 57, 68, 78, 87, 110, 234
Indian temple, 82, 86
Indo-Europeans, 67–68
Indra, 53, 54
Indrashátru, 149–150
Io, 57
Islamic cult, 15
Islamic faith, 14

Japanese aesthetics, 139
Jeffers, Robinson, 15

Jerusalem (Blake), 165, 168, 169
Jesuits, 221
Jesus, 228
John of the Cross, Saint, 217, 218–222, 229
Joshu, 132
Judeo-Christian God, 160
Jung, Carl, 43, 90, 212
Jupiter, 68

Kaaba, 14
Kabir, 48, 56–57, 222
Káto'ya, 194, 195
Keeping Still, 109
Kên, 108, 109
Kenner, Hugh, 44
Kiva, 185
Knoll of Hidden Heights, 120
Knowledge, 120–121
Koan, 42, 128–139, 140, 141–142, 216, 225
Kokyangwuti (Spider Woman), 187
Kópavi, 192, 195
Koran, 14
Krishna, Lord, 56, 222, 239
Kshar, 53
Kshīra. See Language of Sound-Light Continuum; Language of Thought.
Kuskurza, 199

Language, 16, 33ff., 45, 61, 223
  Chinese, 103 ff.
  of Chuang Tzu, 118ff.
  of Eternity, 54, 166–167
  four levels of, 166–177, 228
  pictorial nature of, 103ff.
  reveals and conceals, 76
  of Sound-Light Continuum, 54, 167–171
  of syllables, 60ff.
  of Taoist sages and scientists, 123
  of Thought, 59–60, 171
  Vedic, 51
  of Words, 172ff.
  and Zen, 128–139
Language-games, 131, 157
Languages, 15
  Indo-European, 39, 42
Last Judgment, 235
Latin, 39
Lavaihoya, 194

Lemaître, Abbé Georges Édouard, 23
Leucippus, 160
Light, 58, 76
Lightning, 54, 55, 57, 68, 92
Locke, John, 44
Long Darkness, 58, 75, 76
Lord of All Creatures, 41, 49, 213

Mahākāshyapa, 135–136, 141
Man, 164, 166, 168
Maṇḍala, 91, 139, 167, 168, 169, 174, 176,
    177, 212, 213, 214
Mantra, 42, 51–52, 53, 57, 59, 60, 74, 85,
    128, 139, 141, 216, 225
Maori, 57, 58
Mao Tse-tung, 105
Másaw, 204, 205
Maxwell, James Clerk, 39
Maya, 62
Mecca, 13–14, 87
Medina del Campo, 221
Meditation, 16
Meredith, William, 103
Merton, Thomas, 222–224
Meru, Mount, 175, 235
Middle Speech, 228
Milosz, Czeslaw, 76, 89
Mochni, 194, 195
Monastery of Santa Ana, 221
Montesquier-Avantes, 30
Moses, 22
Most Sacred Mosque, 14
Mother Earth, 190, 194
Mu, 133–134
Muhammad, 14
Mundaka Upanishad, 174
Muslims, 14

Nalanda, 225
Neihardt, John G., 88
Neptune, 160
Newton, Isaac, 37, 38, 39, 158ff., 169–170,
    172, 173
"Newton" (Blake), 158
Nonsense, 120, 129
North Star, 68, 82
Numbakula, 238

Oaks, 66–68, 99, 116–117, 124, 132, 232–
    233, 240
Oglala Sioux, 88

Olson, Charles, 42
Om, 60, 174
One Heart, 193
Oppenheimer, J. Robert, 52

Palängawhoya, 187, 188, 198
Palo santo trees, 25–27
Parmenides, 157
Patañjali, 49, 68, 69, 70, 71, 73, 75, 76, 84,
    94, 95, 109, 139
P'eng-tsu, 119
Philosophy, 15, 44–45
Physics, 39, 122–123, 159ff., 183–185
Plato, 76, 78
Poetics, Vedic, 51ff.
Poetry, 16, 41, 62, 74
Polaris, 68
Pole Star, 68, 69, 70, 71, 73, 75, 76, 79, 83,
    86, 94, 109, 235
Pöqánghoya, 187, 188, 198
Pound, Ezra, 41, 42
Pratello della Giustizia, 235
Prayer, 16, 233
Primal Forms, Two, 106
Primal Pair, 106
"Primitive Like an Orb, A" (Stevens),
    95
Protestant Reformation, 221
Proto-Indo-European language, 39, 40–
    41
Proto-Indo-European oak term (*dorw*),
    67, 68, 75, 174
Proto-Indo-European tribes, 40–41
Psychology, 42–43
Puranas, 74–75
P'u River, 116

Qoyangnoptu, 189

Ramakrishna, 90
Rapallo, 79
Realms, Six, 120
Religion, 14, 130
Renaissance, 235
Republic, The (Plato), 76, 78, 172
Rich in Happiness Tree, 80, 84
Riddles, 53, 129–139
Rigveda, 60
Rishis, 50
River of Life, 169
Russian Orthodox tradition, 228

Samādhi, 70
Samaveda, 60
Samuel, Herbert, 122
samyama, 69, 70
Sanskrit, 39, 42, 52, 53, 58, 70
Satori, 139
Saviors, 174
Scientific thought, 37–39
Seeing Speech (pashyanti), 228
Sekida, Katsuki, 134
Sekitō, 133
Seppo, 133
Shaman, 82, 95
Shamanism, Siberian, 76
Shear, Jonathan, 71, 73, 74, 78, 84
Shelley, Percy Bysshe, 79
Shikhara, 87
Shri Yantra, 85, 94
Shu, 47
Siberia, 78
  shamanism in, 76
Siberian yurt, 82
Siddhi, 69, 95
Signs, 34, 35
Síkangnuqua, 189
Silence, 21, 48, 54, 60, 166
Sinai, 22
Sioux, Oglala. See Oglala Sioux.
Snyder, Gary, 42
Socrates, 172
Soma, 53
"Song of the Soul That Rejoices in Know-
  ing God Through Faith" (Saint John
  of the Cross), 218
Sorcerer of Les Trois Frères. See Trois
  Frères, Sorcerer of, Les.
Sótuknang, 186, 187, 188, 189, 190, 194,
  195, 196, 197, 198, 199, 201, 202, 203
Space, 164, 166, 171
Space-time, 181, 183–185
Sphoṭa, 226
Spider Woman, 180, 181, 186, 187, 188,
  189, 194, 198, 200, 201, 202
Spring and Autumn, 120
Stevens, Wallace, 95
Stone, 16, 20–21, 54, 79, 240
Sun, 53, 54, 74, 180, 189, 190
Sushumna, 80
Sūtras, 42, 69, 74, 94, 109, 141–142, 216,
  225
Swahili, 37

Syllable, 60, 61
Symbolization, 33
Symbolizing, 33
Symbols, 15–16, 173–174
  focal in Western philosophy, 45
  and human mind, 44
  poetic, 39ff.
  psychological, 43–44
  and signs, 34–35

T'ai, Mount, 119
Taiowa, 181, 186, 188
Tálawva, 189, 190, 192
Tao, 106, 107, 114, 117, 122, 124
  of symbols, 16, 37
Taoism, 114ff., 128
Taoists, 114, 115, 116, 123, 239
"Ten Bulls," 142
Teng Yin Fong, 133
Tenryu, 133
Teresa of Ávila, Mother, 221, 222
Terrible Goddess, 176
Teutons, 68
Theories, 15, 16, 37–39, 119
Thoughts, 16
Thrasymachus, 172
Thunder, 55
Thunder Bearer, 68
Thunder God, of Teutons, 68
Tibetan Buddhism, 211
Time, 164, 166, 169, 171, 175
Tokpa, 194–198
Tokpela, 186–194
Tortoise, 116, 157, 172
Tortoise shell, 105
Tree, 67, 76, 82–83, 103, 110, 142
  of Awakening, 87
  of Life, 87
Trigrams, Eight, 106
Trois Frères, Sorcerer of, Les, 31, 32, 45
Trou souffleur, 30
Tungus, 82
Túwaqachi, 187, 203
Two Hearts, 193
"Tyger, The" (Blake), 176

Ultimate Speech (Shabdha-brahman), 228
Uttered Speech (vaikhari), 229

Valabhī, 225
Valéry, Paul, 23

Van den Heuvel, Cor, 139
Vedas, 49–63
Vibratory Centers, 192, 195
Virgin Mother, 237
Virtues, Eight, 120
Vision(s), 15, 50, 53, 88–89, 90, 165
Vritra, 53–54

Wakoski, Diane, 226
Waste Land, The (Eliot), 41, 212, 215
Way and Its Power, The (Lao Tzu), 122
Whitehead, Alfred North, 238
White Waters, 121
Wild-and-Witless, 121
Wittgenstein, Ludwig, 45, 51, 129–132, 157, 227
Word, the, 15, 16, 53, 55, 57, 58, 59, 6off., 76, 110, 166, 167, 171, 172, 175, 177, 211, 212, 213, 214, 215, 216, 225ff., 233

Words, 16, 128
  of Chuang Tzu, 118
  Indo-European, 39–41
  and pictures, 102–103

Yak, 118
Yang, 106, 107, 108, 110
Yantra, 85, 86, 87, 91, 174, 213
Yarrow, 105
Yatsutami, 133
Yellow Emperor, 121
Yepes y Álvarez, Juan de. *See* John of the Cross, Saint.
Yin, 106, 107, 108, 110
Yoga Sūtras, 69

Zen, 34, 128–152, 222–224, 237, 240
Zeno of Elea, 157, 172
Zeus, 68, 98, 160
Zukav, Gary, 120